WAITING FOR MANGO SEASON

ELLIE COOPER

FAVOURITE COW PUBLISHING

DEDICATION

For my uniquely wonderful mother, Jackie.

For John,
To be loved by you was everything.

For Lesley Cooper,
Thank you for the butterflies.

For Layla,
The Best Thing.

Illustrated by Emma Abel

Favourite Cow Publishing

FOREWORD

The messiness has come out
just like she said it would.
Like a tangled knot or a spluttering engine,
which, when oiled
became smooth again,
you slowed my heartbeat, India.
Two years in this land has slowed my heartbeat.

ARRIVAL

*The sweat runs down my neck and rubs against a heavy backpack,
overloaded for my two-month long journey. White storks sit
patiently as if painted, dotted among the long-stemmed grasses and
rubble. Two elderly men share a moment, masala chai in tiny cups.*

*You rush by, India, too quickly from the seat of this rickshaw, the
driver impatient, and I, covering my nose and mouth with my
scarf, am ecstatic to get out of the airport and into the streets. The
beeping and the incessant chatter of the road vehicles, which seem
to say, "I'm here".*

*Small, squat, fat, sweet bananas piled on trucks; the colour of them
makes my eyes water. Imperfect and battered, they are a far cry
from plastic-wrapped neighbours across the sea.*

*Home. It seems impossible that this morning I was wondering if I
should come at all. As my tongue settles in my un-brushed mouth,
and chapped lips smack together, I glance at a group of women,
glam and pristine in crisp white shirts and Birkenstocks, who click*

and clack their fingers to skinny young men to carry their bags for a pittance. I, harem-panted and bug-sprayed, clutching hand sanitiser and a charity-shop copy of Lonely Planet, take my first steps onto the Indian soil and cry silent tears of joy.

GOA

The moon is still the same moon, but these tree trunks stretch as wide as oceans. Banyan trees. I whisper their name, let it walk on my tongue, watch their branches dangle tall streams of tangles over quiet footpaths, as I walk through the villages of incense, past the fires of dried cow dung.

The dry grass, coaxed into the mud by sandalled feet, grows sparsely and is rough to the touch. The trees narrow, and all the sounds of the jungle are here, strange, and overwhelming.

Threadbare clothes in many colours hang on lines between tiny mud houses, the wind painting them burnt orange with dirt. Butterflies settle on leaves of jungle green that line the beaches of pebbled shells, vermillion flowers fluttering across my feet. Bats screech in clusters in the branches overhead, signalling that sunset is about to begin.

Ten sleeping cows are nestled baking in balmy heat, yawning and warm and looking out at the ocean. Coloured boats wait their turn

*on the edge of the sand, dragged ashore by the rough hands of
fishermen waiting for the tide.
I decide I shall become a collector of sunsets; I race to catch the
first. The sun is rose-gold tonight, a perfect pastel picture.*

*Onto the sand I step, coming to rest among coconuts strung from
the rafters, gently knocking, and clinking in our ears. Shells rattle
and swing, structures creak in the gentle wind, and there is not
another sound but for the soft reggae on the stereo, and that sea.
The sand stretches for miles with the gentle curve of the bay.*

*Around the cove I watch and wait as pinky-orange hues turn to
purest gold. The ruffle atop the tide is pleasing to the eye,
mesmerising, like melted chocolate poured slowly over crispy wafers
in shiny advertisements, lapping over and over.*

*I nestle in a deckchair serenaded by bartenders jamming the same
old five songs on guitar, the scent of marijuana on the air, incense,
and the sight of a thousand stars. In the blackness, a single voice
rings out, singing a sublime Indian melody,
"Ong Namo Guru Dev Namo."
(Bow to the divine teacher within)
-Adi Mantra*

GAGORI

Fans stopped and started again as power ebbed and flowed through the little village. I rented a small room for four English pounds per night, with a dripping tap and a bust windowpane that peeled away from the frame, so that I had to bend it back into place to stop the blood-drunk mosquitoes from finding their way in. I tucked the sides of my Deet-sprayed net into my bed sheet and taped up every cigarette hole with duct tape, which fell off again in the heat. I lathered myself in sun cream, factor fifty mixed with insect repellent, wiped down my cutlery with hand gel and jumped at the crickets which lived in the bathroom drain.

I was thrilled to be experiencing it all, but I was filled with a fear that shouted at me loudly, and daily. Perhaps I would catch some terrible disease, or would succumb to some injury, or would get sick from water or food. I brushed my teeth with bottled water, did not dare to try the salad, and washed my hands constantly. My guidebook had made it clear; India was a different world, and I did not know any of it.

I followed a snaking path into the jungle to find a small

dwelling in the trees. I wiped my brow and looked around at the other trainees. They looked every bit as pale and foreign as I, swatting at flies and sweating profusely, as we waited for our teacher. The four-week long 'healing massage' course that I was about to begin was my initial reason for travelling to India.

Gagori, proprietor and tutor at Aithein school, looked at you with eyes that did not care for artifice. She dressed simply and spoke plainly and had a steadiness about her that was quite disarming, with arms stronger than iron. She was a little thing, petite and with long glossy black hair and the most wonderful skin that hinted at her being many years younger than her age. Despite her initial smile and a soft welcome, she had a hardness about her that made me instantly want to melt it, to see if she would become gooey and respond in saccharine sweetness; but Gagori was not to be broken like some horse in a stable; Gagori was to be earned.

On our first day, she encouraged all practitioners to partake in their own therapy and try to heal any stuck emotions that needed addressing before laying their hands on others. It became clear that this would be meaningful work.

Our February mornings consisted of anatomy lessons in a yoga shala on a hill, learning the names of muscles and bones under the gecko-covered, palm-branched roof. We learnt which muscle groups were hotspots for emotions, and how to open them with our touch. She asked us to stand in front of each other without our clothes, reading our faces and bodies, so that we could look for misalignments to correct on the table. The Tai Chi class on the beach, at five-thirty o'clock in the morning, was a mixture of discipline, beauty, and irritation, trying to focus our minds on stillness.

As the days leaked into late, sweaty afternoons, I learnt

7

how to coax muscles into relaxation, gliding palms and fingertips across calves and navels and shoulders. I circled the massage table, remembering Gagori's meditative Tai Chi steps, breathing slowly, bare footed, and with my eyes closed, I lost myself in hours and days of massage as I caressed and smoothed away the hurt of not only others but of myself. It was dancing, therapy, and meditation, all in one.

As someone on my table started to cry, I pushed a little deeper into the spot I was working on. I watched them take a deep breath and release whatever they had been holding on to. It was magic. The area around the trapezius now felt different; it was no longer as rigid, the lactic acid had dispersed, as bubbles that now felt alive under my fingers crackled and popped. This work was more than just muscles and bones, ligaments, and tendons. It was doing everyone a world of good.

I wondered what on earth I had been doing, throwing myself into high stress career positions. I wondered if I could make a life which allowed me to change that. I had never been away from England for longer than two weeks, I was always in a cycle of pay check to pay check, never saving and living to my means. I had a payment plan for an expensive vacuum cleaner which I did not remember buying, to tidy a house which was never really lived in. I had no idea where the last five years had gone, eating, sleeping, working, repeating, but I wanted them back.

I thought about how my teaching job in the UK felt like an Indian pressure cooker, and how I was always waiting for the whistle, a release which never came, a pressure which only continued to build. My students, a class of teenagers with mixed disabilities, were the highlight of my day. They loved me and I them, but the job was difficult, a never-ending fight for their wellbeing in a system which did not understand them. I worried who would take care of them like I could if I ever worked up the courage to leave.

I realised this could be applied to many other parts of my life: my long-term relationship, my geriatric cat, my mother. I did not know what they would do without me, but I knew I was unfulfilled and unhappy. I was looking for a different kind of existence, which did not revolve around which new Netflix show was on or accepting one more pint in the pub on a Friday night.

It is said that those who want to help others are best at putting themselves last. To help us, Gagori created circles of truth-telling in which everyone was heard in completion, no matter the duration of their story. We did not give advice; we were only heard. This became hours of habit-breaking, pattern-changing, shame-shaking wake-up calls to most of us. For me, it was clear that I had a lot of changes to make, because there I was, in paradise, and all I could seem to do was complain about how hard my life was.

As the group told their stories, some of them upset me. I cried along with them.

Gagori was known for the pearls of wisdom that came from her lips. She had a way of looking at you and telling you what you really needed to hear. I saw Gagori out of the corner of my eye and she was watching me intently; her look was not friendly. She asked me why I was crying.

"I have always felt people's pain," I suggested.

Gagori said calmly,

"You take in so much of others' pain when you are ignoring your own. You must look inwards to find the source of your own pain before helping others."

She grinned as she told us that everything in life was our choice in some way, that we had the power to change anything that we wanted to, and that when we blamed others for our misfortune, we only created more stories to tell, that would make us unhappy.

Gagori shrugged,

"When you point the finger, three of the fingers are pointing back at you."

She laughed. We laughed. It was true.

Waiting for sunset one evening, I watched a large dog stalk a woman from afar. I saw what was about to happen before she did, his jaws glistening, the sudden quickening of his step, the angle his neck took as he hunted her. Quick as a flash I clapped my hands loudly, as I had seen the locals do, and my relief for her faded as quickly as it came, for instead of attacking this woman, he turned immediately around and approached me, and my friend who was by my side. We threw sand at the dog, and it loped off, but as I laughed it off nervously my friend looked at me sternly and with anger shaking in her voice, said:

"You brought harm to not only yourself but to me. At that moment, to save someone else whom you do not know, you placed the harm back onto you. Why do you do that? I want you to see how you choose to offer yourself so much of other people's pain."

I was dumbfounded. What my teacher was trying to show me was the same, but these words stung more because I had almost injured someone else, too. I saw how I was in a pattern of taking others' issues and making them my own, like an addiction to conflict, like I was a rescuer when in truth I could not even rescue myself.

After that, the truth circles in our classroom began to affect me less and less. I no longer cried at their stories, no longer felt anger rise in my chest at their bitter injustices, I no longer felt my stomach grip in anguish at their collective losses in life. I decided to turn all my attention inwards. It felt terribly selfish, but I turned off my phone and let the messages from home pile up. With this, some quietness came.

We chanted mantras, and the universal sound of 'Aum'. By chanting Aum, it is said that the mind becomes aligned with the breath and allows a person to get into an elevated state of consciousness which Hindus call Samadhi. This brings the material mind under control and enables you to access spiritual realisations. For me, it was my first step towards being able to meditate. The vibrations on my lips and tongue moved to my forehead, and the tips of my fingers. I was in complete relaxation, for probably the first time in my life.

India would change me in every way, starting with switching off my mind and slowing down my whole body. Gagori had given me the tools I needed, and now it was up to me to practice my Sadhana, a daily spiritual meditation to help me find inner peace.

"The messiness will come out," Gagori smiled, "It is like India. There is much that is mess, but still, it is beautiful."

LIFE FORKS

Life can have many forks in the road. I had planned to travel to Canada some months before my India trip, but it was curtailed. If I had achieved that life goal, I would not have been in India when the world locked down, and my life may have taken a very different turn. I believe it was the doing of the universe.

The fork that I took after leaving Gagori and Goa was the first step towards big change. The urge to take the left fork, to stay with my community and remain in the bubble of what we had created together, was very strong. Had I done so, I do not think I would have learnt very much at all. Sometimes, to stay where you are comfortable does not allow for exponential growth.

The call that I felt towards the city of Varanasi was like a hard kick to my stomach, forcing me onto the right path, and the unknown. One of India's oldest cities and a pilgrimage spot where many journey to die, I knew that this was the city that would show me the rawness of India. I wanted to see the dead bodies burn. Perhaps it was the end of a cycle, the burning of my patterns and chapters; perhaps it was time to lay my troubles to rest. A journey to Varanasi is said to 'invite' death, and perhaps this was the case, a death of various parts of myself. Whatever the reason, I set out to the holy city alone, to try to find whatever I had been searching for my whole life.

With both feet propped against the open door, I pushed my back against cold metal with the wind blowing in my hair and the ever-changing country flashing by.

Slowing down into stations, the farmlands made way for rubble and discarded waste, the colours accentuating the sunset as cityscapes engulfed the skies and became silhouettes. As the train dawdled through slums, the morning line of men squatted bare bottomed at station platforms, leaning in between stopped carriageways to hock and spit. The call of the tea sellers, chai wallahs, came, interrupting dreamy sleep of those rocked to unconsciousness by lumbering carriages, the squeal of brakes on rails, the jangling of keys in the porters' pockets, and train announcers' mumbled rhetoric through slatted windows.

The piles of people in the cheaper parts of the train were crammed in tightly, some on the laps of others, some sitting in the luggage racks up high, or sleeping in the galley for hurried feet to step over. The toilets changed in luxury, from western-style lavatories to simple, open slats in the floor where the rails underneath could be seen flashing between squatting feet.

The metal jugs used for cleaning oneself were chained to the wall, filled from the tap. The carriages with seating and air conditioning were devoid of feeling somehow, like the personality of the train depends entirely on the close quarters of the train-folk. Those cold carriages of silence and squeaky-clean glass windows simply do not tell the same story, a little reminiscent of European journeys in comfort, without the complimentary biscuit packets.

VARANASI

He has no teeth, but takes the chocolate anyway, sucking it with a
wide smile. A herd of cows and an old man with a stick stand in
our way in the blistering midday heat. We speed past cheerful
billboards and brilliantly green fields that bank the road, leading to
Varanasi. Lop-eared goats are tied to bits of old pipe, a small boy
squats to shit through a crack in the pavement, businessmen read
newspapers under the shade of a Banyan tree, sipping cups of Chai.

The streets change. Fervent and swarming, the colours turn
brighter. Scrawny chickens peck at cages too small to contain them,
dogs whine and children scream at each other as horns sound so
loud it makes my ears squeeze shut. A cow twitches silently, its neck
broken, hanging on.

A lady sits cross-legged in a lime green sari, matching her fruit in
her lap. Bananas hang in long columns, cut down with a pocketknife.
The streets are a jumble of smoke and petrol-flavoured air, winding
bikes and crammed tuk-tuks and flaps of carpet, rug, and fabric.

I stop at a street cart; sour lime Pani Puri stings my senses and one after another I swallow them whole, my mouth a screaming fire of ecstasy and taste and spice. A seller laughs. He takes pity on me and gives me a sweet one, potato and plum juice, my eyes rimmed red but gleaming, my lips a cherry pink and cheeks aflame.

I smell the earthy scent of the Ganges before I see it. I wind through the throngs of people and settle into a rowing boat, floating on a sea of black-brown murk.
The Aarti begins[1]. A lucky few hold a long rope, and ring bells that stretch across the Ghat[2] and we watch as chosen men, gifted with patience and perfect movements from their father's fathers hold gigantic flames and heavy candles, throwing them over their heads with their cores as strong as iron. They swing smoking sage, the air full of incense and song, chanting,
"Aum Shanti, Shanti, Shanti[3]."

Petals and blossom fill the air and land at our feet, as droplets of polluted water extinguish candles and vermillion powder is placed on foreheads with fragrant sandalwood. Boats clack together bound with simple rope, and the gentle hum of the crowd gathers to a roar.

I watch the boat man plunge wooden oars into black water. He told me they found a stillborn child in the earliest hours of the misty morning, frozen on the steps down to the water's edge. He told me a woman in white came to carry it away, blessed it, and did not give it to the Ganges, too innocent to be burned or sunk with a stone. And yet it is beautiful, birth and death at the edge of this river, she who gives life and holds the grey dregs of old, a thick vein of hope to many, that still shimmers under dark skies, when the moon is just right.

---

1. Aarti: A religious ritual of worship, in which light and songs are offered to various deities.
2. Ghat: The steps down to the water.
3. Aum: In Buddhism, Hinduism and Jainism, Aum or 'Om' is the first syllable, the first sound of the universe, and as such is often chanted to bring connection to everything.
   Shanti: Peace

FUNERALS

Cries of "Ram Nam Satya Hai," echo into the distance, and I feel the cold. The February morning here is brisk, but it is not the chill in the air that haunts me, it is the deep melancholy of the street, the historic pounding of footsteps of those who came before me; so many lives, so many carried souls, and it feels as if it is filled with ghosts.

On the walk down to the water's edge, the funeral processions came quickly, one after the other, announcing themselves over the heads of the crowd. The mourners chanted in a low, rhythmic tone, carrying their dead on a bed of fabric and wood.

I watched two exhausted mourners; they shouldered a lost loved one from many miles away, in the next town. The bodies were decorated in white, red, and orange flowers, sandalwood paste, and jewellery. As they passed, I saw the faces of each of the dead, black kohl on their eyes.

I sat on the edge of Manikarnika ghat, frozen in awe, as I stared at the piles of ash and the black grates on which they placed body after body to be set alight. I took a deep breath and shuffled nearer, filled with a desperate curiosity.

The families looked worn. They have waited three hours for their dead, watching flames make light work of a lifetime.

I had sat through many funerals in England. Black umbrellas drenched with rain, wearing something conservative bought especially for the occasion, veiled hats, plastic packs of tissues, no mascara. The silence deafening on the entry to the crematorium, as people shuffle to take their seats on hard wooden benches in a cold room with a stained carpet. Herded through in fifteen-minute windows, with a squeaky wall-bracket holding a spluttering ten-inch screen, featuring the Windows XP logo or a skewed list of names; timings of the dead. I could never take my eyes off those screens.

That a lifetime can be reduced to this, I thought, an impersonal time slot, and the same old format; a too-cheery speaker with a forced smile and an overly calm voice and an ineffectual microphone on a broken lead that crackles with every uttered word.

"A lovely service."

"Yes, it was."

Three thousand years and many a hand have stoked a fire that never burns out, in its small grate. An elderly woman with whisper-thin wrinkled skin lights the elephant grass one by one. It licks along the long stems and is transferred to the pyres. She looks at me carefully, placing ash from the fire on my forehead, and I shudder with the enormity of her gesture. They tell me that she sits patiently all her life for her turn at the fire to be passed to another. Her watch will soon be over.

It is touching, watching palms touch feet of ashes and then their hearts, fingers to foreheads. I see a ripped-apart torso and then the empty face of one who is carried to the water. One by one I hear the skulls pop, the collective sighs of relief as the families listen to the soul escape. My eyes meet skin melting from bone. Brains drip from an open crevice as a grandfather tells me that after all this adorning, the fancy jewellery means nothing.

Dogs fight on the ground for scraps of meat, but there are only piles of bones to lick clean. I expect to smell more. There is singed hair, but otherwise nothing but smoke, and the wind, and the ever-present cow dung that lines the steps, where we wait, for yet another body.

We often close the curtains on our dead in England. The way we hide it; that all-important final moment so tastefully sparing us from the reality of it. The thought of our demise remains ever-frightening, as we walk away thanking our Gods that it was not us this time. Our grief is hidden, too, inside blacked-out windows of hearses to cry behind the glass. The vehement anger when someone does not stand still as the procession passes by, discussed afterwards at the pub wake, where landlords charge hundreds of pounds for cheap sandwiches and soggy crisps.

As I stood at Manikarnika Ghat, I watched one father take the ashes of his son's feet onto his tongue and swallow them. The intimacy of the gesture choked me.

Families nodded at me as they saw me and invited me to stand with their dead. They patiently explained their thirteen-day long rituals with pride and great reverence to a white woman with no ties to their Gods. They took my hands, smiling. They told me that they knew that their loved ones had attained Moksha, or liberation from the cycle of birth and death, a relief for them all. Hindus believe that the soul travels from one body to another, and that when you have learnt enough to let go of the desires, anger, frustrations, and fears in your life, you can achieve 'Artha', which means 'goal'. If you do not learn enough in one life, your soul will be reborn until you do.

What a life, I thought, *to live only in the pursuit of total peace.*

Humbled, I tugged my scarf closer over my head and bowed my head to my hands and then my heart, as another body was carried out to the grey-topped water, dried and lit and mourned for with not one single tear. In this land, death was an achievement.

By discovering another culture, I now perceived somewhat of a lack in my own education around death. Varanasi had gifted me the visceral, gutting truths of my impending demise; the finality of it all mixed in with a sense of peace and hope. If death had always been shrouded in mystery, then being able to see the final step allowed me to see past the fear of it.

Something clicked into place that day. The Burning Ghat was grotesque, but it was also stunningly beautiful. It was exactly what I had needed to see. I found a flask of courage on a grey set of steps, with the ashes of many fluttering in the wind.

INDIAN RAILWAYS

I boarded a train to the South, and sat outside the carriage of 3ac, in my favourite spot, with the wind blowing tendrils of blonde hair into my face. I held on, a well-thumbed paperback in one hand, and the other on the rail, and closed my eyes.

The old carriages often have little quirks. Between the open train doors at the end of the carriages, is a compartment for the porters to sleep at night, in the wall itself. Under this is a clasp which, when shifted, will let down a bed in the side of the wall which can be used to sit on when looking out of the open door. Not many will sit here, preferring instead to stay with luggage or in their assigned seat, but not I; it is the perfect way to see the idiosyncrasies of India.

The fun that is to be had on Indian trains; the risk in hopping out as the train is still rolling to squeeze through open gaps, remembering your carriage number, as chai wallahs pour steaming liquid into paper cups, ladling chickpeas and dal onto doughy chapatis, sprinkling fresh green chillies as garnish. Pani[1] bottles or sugary mango juice are thrust into eager hands to wash down the spice, with long purple packets of biscuits, shiny packets of dried, crispy lentils, moong dal. Some stations have rare jewels; a samosa stand, piping hot and morning made, greasy and packaged in a newspaper.

Long journeys, taking days at a time, rely mainly on these tiny stalls. Time is short and express trains often slow their pace by stations without stopping, meaning that a jump out of the doors from these steps means a quick dash to a cart, catching the end of the train again.

"Train food is not palatable," families would tell me, and I would nod in agreement as plastic-covered thalis[2] were offered to me, just-warm, sealed and beige-looking. I have now taken enough Indian trains to know; the real adventure is in the catching of dinner, just in time, rupees and newspapered treats thrown into snatching fists, whilst tumbling over fellow humans at the tureens, shouting, "Dhanyavaad, Ji!"[3] as the train whisks you away once more.

---

1. Pani: Water
2. Thalis: meaning, 'large plate'.
3. Dhanyavaad Ji: 'Thank you, Sir.'

THE LOCKDOWN

The Lockdown was whispered all over India, and suddenly the fear came like the onslaught of a bad cold, like a bad taste in your mouth, as rumours of a virus began to spread like Monsoon fever[1] in July.

I had made it to Kerala, about to embark on a month-long yoga course, with a teacher who was so intense that he put me into Pincha on my first day, a scorpion-shaped yoga pose, dropping me on my neck and telling me to 'walk it off' by doing twenty 'Chaturanga' push-ups. Whether the universe was trying to prevent me from getting permanent brain damage or not, Kerala started to shut down the very next day.

The change was palpable. There were hurried footsteps, locals practically hissed at foreigners and Varkala beach was empty, with a sign that said 'Stay out of the ocean'; upon asking a police officer, I was told that Covid was in the sea and that if we went in, we would catch it. There was no point in arguing, as I realised that if this was the extent of the hysteria on day one, then it could only get much worse.

In the next few hours, flights began to disappear from

travel sites, and my yoga friends were preparing to hunker down in our Shala, or yoga hall, and create a community. This was a beautiful idea, but I was decided; the forty-degree heat and reactions from the locals were enough for me to withdraw my eight hundred pounds deposit and at four o'clock that morning, I sat bolt upright in bed, my intuition shouting like a war drum in the very core of me, and I went to wake the girl in the room below mine.

"I'm going to the North," I said. "Do you want to come? I think it's our best chance. If we're going to be trapped in India, I want to be in the mountains, far away from everyone."

She didn't even hesitate, and we stayed awake, packing our belongings, and taking the first taxi to the airport that morning. It was just in time; as we arrived at Trivandrum airport the displays were flashing madly with cancellations and delays, and we found out that they had cancelled flights out of Kerala, with ours being one of only four flights still flying. We did not uncross our fingers until we were finally in the air, knowing full well that we still had Delhi to contend with.

---

1. Monsoon fever: The fever refers to water-borne illnesses which strike when the rains come.

DELHI

As I throw my bags into the back of what I thought was a Tuk-tuk, I notice in the darkness that it is not what I thought, but is a ramshackle seat strapped to a bicycle. I am not going far, five minutes on the map, and the cool of the evening entices me to this open carriage ride.

I am shocked to see a man of about sixty-five, though he could have been older, mount the bike with some difficulty and start to pedal through the busy streets. My Hindi is not good enough to protest; I try, a startled cry snatching at my throat, but he is strong-legged and seems to be doing this with ease.

The shame comes then, burning at my face as I realise my privilege, and suddenly I do not want to be seen at all, but I purposely do not hide my eyes from others, knowing I deserve their stares. No-one blinks an eye at a white woman in a carriage, but I weep, the enormity of it engulfing me, as I feel like a master with a whip. I think of my mother in England of the same age as him, and what back-breaking work this is for such little pay. I cannot bear it; I

*know not what he earns, but it is night-time and getting colder, him
in a threadbare kurta.*

*We hit a steep hill and I groan and clutch at my chest as he does not
hear my protestations. I want to get out. I want to put him in the
back and pedal myself, wanting so badly to take the load for us
both. The road flattens out, and my heart stops smashing into itself
in anguish. I press a two hundred rupee note into his hand; four
times what this was worth, but it is still not enough. He blinks,
unsure. He is an honest man.*

*I wipe dark Delhi tear-tracks off my road-blackened face and take
my own loaded bags up four flights of hotel stairs, to the shock of
three porters. Not again. Not tonight. I exhale the inexplicable need
to take his struggle as my own, knowing he is not mine to save.
As I wave him goodbye with my hands pressed tightly in thanks, I
see his hip bones jutting out, the frailness of him, and wish I had
done more.*

ESCAPE FROM THE AIRPORT

Delhi was packed. The panic of the pandemic had spread across the north of the country much faster than in the south, as news came from the capital. There was not an inch of space on the floor, and every seat was taken. Everything was delayed by many hours, and as we received our emergency rations which our airline handed to every passenger, we began to believe that we might be stuck in Delhi for the entire lockdown.

People slept heads to feet, women with women and men with men. I took up a place next to the window and tucked myself in, earphones in against the noise. I was on watch, eyes glued to the departures board. Finally, our gate turned green, and I grabbed my friend and our bags and ran to board, white-masked assailants barging in at every available space. The earlier flights which had been cancelled were allowed to board this one, and it was first come, first served. There was no way I was missing this flight, as I thought of freedom and that beautiful river and mountain home which I had only pictured, but which I somehow knew would keep me safe.

MA GANGA

*I stand with my arms on the bridge over Rishikesh, holding tight to
the cable, peering down at the perfect crystalline water below. I
suck air into my lungs like I am surfacing from a deep dive. On the
rocks, locals wash their feet, faces, armpits, hands, a simple towel
around their waists. They do not use soap; the Ganges is their life
source, a Goddess, and they will not taint her. How they bend and
break and pray to her, Ma Ganga, three times ducking their heads
in, held noses.*

*I finally place my feet in India's most beloved river, at the ghat
which is painted butter yellow. The water is shining. Varanasi was
black water, oil, ashes, and discarded match packets; a river of filth,
and they all knelt and drank it. I cup my hand and drink the water
here. It has no taste, like drinking air. The Ganga is freezing, but it
is like a breath through my soul, and I shiver. The sun bakes on my
back, stronger than I had imagined in these mountains.*

*An eagle flies, circling, riding the thermals, and on and up to the
mountains, which tower impressively around this sheltered home.
Rishikesh. Temples of pink, orange and white, set into the hills, the*

rapids ferocious, catching the current into a thunderous roar,
beaten against the rocks.

I watch for sunset. I am rewarded with the first of many; burnt
orange sky and whispered clouds of grey slate. The water turns still.
Tiny whirlpools open and gargantuan fish make a meal of the tiny
flies on the water, leaping with great aplomb. Monkeys scatter and
push their young off the rocks, alarming the street dogs who lie at
our feet. A chase begins and with baring of teeth and red nipples,
they clamber and crash into the trees above, and chide their young.

Someone strikes a chord on a battered guitar, as choruses of
mantras ring out clear as bells across the now flat, patient river. It
is time now, and as the sun sets people put their heads to their
hands and hearts and sit in collective silence. A distant peacock
calls, a monkey chirps, and bats swoop over our heads.

One by one, many feet start to gather up their belongings to make
the journey home, but I will stay here until the last chink of light
fades and my mind is clear, and I have filled my ears with the sweet
sound of stillness.

TO SAFETY

The lockdown, though imminent, was handled entirely differently in Rishikesh. From the moment I arrived, the calm was like a warm hug, the airport deserted, and the air felt like a crisp piece of heaven in my lungs; I could breathe. I immediately took off my mask and took deep gulps of air which was not filled with panic.

I threw myself into the cold Ganga, cleansing myself of the entire journey, the terror I had felt in those around me and the heaviness of the south, shaking it off and sending it downstream. I laughed as I shivered and hopped about to get warm in the early March temperature and thought about how Covid was certainly not in this river, this town, that already felt like a secure home to me in these uncertain times.

I began to look for something meaningful to do with my time and thought about resuming my yoga, but all yoga schools were gently closing with the news from Delhi leaking in.

A friend of mine, from my home in the UK, appeared as if by magic, not least because the last that I had heard of him was that he was eating out of supermarket bins in Turkey, and he recommended a Tantra[1] course here in India, which I was about to join. Aidan had left the UK some years ago in favour of a more nomadic life and had returned home barefoot and speaking very slowly and vaguely. At the time, it was alarming to me, to watch him renounce all his previous worldly treasures and to have seemingly changed so much, but now I understood that he was living even more authentically than before. I hugged him and stood back to admire him; India suited him and had softened him even further.

The Tantra course ran for three full days before it was shut down as well, but by the end of that short time, I had met a community, and I was no longer so alone.

The Tantra course taught a basic introduction; this practice believes that everything is a duality and is connected in a divine dance, the sun and moon, masculine and feminine energies, life and death, love and hate. We spent our time eye-gazing and dancing, learning which chakras, or energy points, to open with a corresponding yoga pose. It took me time to shake off the embarrassment of the eye gazing, and I realised then how blocked I was, how scared I was of true intimacy if I could not look into another's eyes without smirking. I wondered if that was growing up in England, or if it was just me.

As we danced to live music in a tiny shack, word passed along the street of the impending lockdown that had finally caught up with the North. We knew that it would be the last night in a long time where we would ever feel this free again or would be in a crowded room.

Six months later, we would still be unable to sit together publicly in a restaurant or hug openly in the street, along with the rest of the world.

33

1. Tantra: The belief that everything in the universe is interconnected. There are two strands of Tantra, Buddhist and Hindu. Tantra is seen to expand your consciousness through studying of the ancient texts and by applying the principles to your life. It is a complex subject which uses many different practices to reach your 'highest self'.

LEARNING TO MEDITATE

"You must learn to sit with yourself." – Gagori

We spoke in tongues. Nonsense spewed from our lips for minutes at a time, and still, my mind ran like a hamster wheel; am I doing this right, am I thinking too much, am I controlling the syllables that fall from my lips? Babbling. First the A's, and the B's; why is it in order? I try a W, from the end of the alphabet, and it feels good. The combinations start, D's and Z's merge with vowel sounds. Spit forms at the corners of my mouth and I let it sit there, eyes closed, hands in a Mudra, legs crossed in lotus.

My neck hurts. I roll it around as more nonsense comes, and the hilarity with it, the urge to laugh at the ridiculousness of this moment. I laugh, loudly, and then comes a song, as the urge to chant comes, and I take a breath and sing in a key that does not exist, lamenting to a God I do not know the name of.

A bell rings and we are pushed quickly onto the flats of our backs, lying across a cushion in total ecstasy. Everything goes black and suddenly there are a million stars. I see each one, I see the link; these are my thoughts, this is my anxious mind. There are too many stars and too many thoughts to name them all.

And so, I start to put them out, lights fizzling and popping from my sight until there are fewer of them. A bell rings, again, and we sit back in front of our meditation master. I am crying.

SHUT IN

"Lokah Samastah Sukhino Bhavantu"
(May all beings be happy and be free)
-Indian Mantra

The lockdown arrived quickly in the night in Rishikesh, and suddenly most of us were shut in our houses, physically locked in, with police stationed in the streets. The night before, I had purchased a little heating element for fifty rupees, which remains the most casually dangerous albeit useful piece of Indian equipment imaginable, fond of starting electrical fires and melting into the side of the cups they were supposed to heat. We bought 'Maggi' noodles, the Indian staple, and teabags, and hoarded fruit from the sellers who would also have to leave the streets the next morning.

The proprietor of my hotel was immensely terrified of this impending shut-in and sat at the reception desk transfixed, watching the Indian news channels for all hours of the night. My room did have a tiny balcony, but it was wrought with monkeys. Without a weapon to defend myself against sharp teeth, my chances of seeing daylight were scuppered, and instead I slept a lot, succumbed to watching movies and made instant noodles. The red-faced monkeys of Rishikesh were not to be reckoned with, I had heard.

On the second day, I broke into the roof space.

I found a door at the top of the stairs to watch a great storm that had arrived. They had boarded it with a small scrap of wood; perhaps against Covid, perhaps against these enormous beasts that guarded my doorway, but I had seen a way to freedom, and I was not going to rest until I had at least glimpsed the sky that I had run to so eagerly. I shifted four stained mattresses and prized the 'lock' apart with the hammer they had left directly next to it. I chuckled at the trusting and lackadaisical attitude of Indians that I had come to know so well, and took my first steps into slamming rain, battling winds, and freedom.

It was a purple sky, lightning coming down in terrifying bolts all around me. I had never experienced a storm in the mountains before, and the very real feeling that I was about to die up there came over me with every flash. I watched it hit buildings in the distance, trees in the jungle, and with each crack of thunder I covered my ears, as it was so close.

Indra, God of weather, was making himself known tonight. The storms continued for the next few nights as if in pathetic fallacy, the foreboding of what was to come the next few months for a huge part of the world. For our community, though, that sense of darkness and despair never came.

ROOFTOPS OF RISHIKESH

On the third day of the lockdown, I was out of my bed as soon as I opened my eyes, and I ran to see if the rooftop door had been fixed. It had not.

I decided to call my mother from the roof and asked about home and learnt then to my surprise that the UK had been dealing with this for weeks already, and were depressed, bored and lonely, many contained in city flats without outside spaces of their own. The panic was evident in her voice.

I saw photos of deserted streets and looked up at my surroundings, my freedom, the sky, the monkeys in the trees. I had made the right decision not to go back to my home-land. If I was to be trapped, this was as good a place as any. The locals had ignored the lockdown rules and continued their cricket matches behind my hotel, and I would watch in amusement as they ran in the narrow streets to catch the ball or went to retrieve it from someone's roof.

For most, it was seen as a temporary inconvenience, and the people of Rishikesh really believed that the river Ganga, that rushing, gleaming divide between us and the bigger cities, and the self-sustaining nature of the township and nearby farmers, would ensure that we were kept safe in our bubble for as long as it was needed. It felt hopeful, safe, and most of all, no one was pointing fingers at anyone. With no one new coming into town, the roads barricade off and the river separating us from the main cities, we had created a bubble against the virus. We were all in it together, tourists and locals doing their bit here and there to keep the peace and placate the police. In a world full of panic, Rishikesh was very calm.

As I peered over the edge of my balcony, I saw the whole town of Rishikesh on their rooftops doing yoga or hanging out washing, cooking on small fires in the open air. There was no air of depression here, no fear, and no uncertainty. In a country such as India where deadly diseases are still a problem and people live in slums, there was much more to worry about than being locked in for a few days, or a virus, for that matter. I grinned down at the cows and monkeys and dogs playing and roaming free below me; the street had come alive with animals.

That evening, at sunset, everyone took drums, sound bowls, pots and pans and whatever they had handy up to the top of their buildings and drummed across all of Rishikesh. Like the UK would soon go on to clap for the nurses in their national health service, India was drumming negative vibrations away from the very beginning. The town of Rishikesh believed that the collective vibrations would keep us safe, and I was inclined to believe it too. I cried tears of gratitude as I banged an old paint tin with a wooden stick, as the sense of community and love and hope washed over me.

I was feeling lonely in the huge hotel, but I was lucky that I had two partners in crime just over the road. After three days of noodles and ginger tea, I was desperate to escape and convinced my friends to come and break me out of my boiling hot hotel and roof by lifting the shutters just enough that I could sneak under. I crouched in wait for the police who came by in droves at five-minute intervals, and the minute they had turned their backs, quick as a flash I escaped to the other side of the street and into the arms of my mates. We would eat thali together every evening, while they laughed at my exclamations of real tin plates and cutlery.

Their situation was very different, in a small yoga training studio that had a kitchen and a hall, with huge balconies and a chess-playing yogi in charge. This soon became my temporary home: the soulless wallpaper and harsh strip lighting of my bedroom in stark contrast to yogic teachings on the walls, comfy yoga bolsters, and the company of good men.

The juice stand was everyone's saviour. At seven o'clock in the mornings, after the fruit sellers returned, we waited patiently for the doors of our houses to be unlocked for our three-hour break in curfew. We would wander down to stand on the chalk-marked circles leading along the street to the colourful ladies with their steel hand-squeezing juice machine, and sample exotic fruits such as pomegranate, lychee, guava and amla, in whatever mix was being given out that day. The Indian government may have locked down the towns and cities, but in the mountains the farmers were right next door, so we were very lucky.

Determined not to get sick, our group used the juice cart as an excuse with the police to meet once a day and although we did not hug in the street for fear of upsetting locals, we would take our juices around the corner and cuddle each other secretly, everyone solidly wrapped in mountain blankets, sleepy-eyed. This was my sole purpose for getting out of bed each morning, and it was this kind of soul motivation that kept us all in such high spirits.

We felt like naughty school children as we found more and more places that were staying open in secret to feed the trapped foreigners; our favourite restaurant would close their doors but open around the back to present us with home-cooked food, which, after those initial days of noodles, tasted incredible.

One restaurant bravely put its light on for a minute or so to alert foreigners. There were five of us staying nearby watching out of our windows. We would wait for it and sneak there, under the cover of darkness. We would slip across the police-patrolled street one at a time, melting into the shadows, our backs to the walls upon hearing a motor. We were allowed to sit at tables in only silence and candle-light, ordering in hushed voices. The very thing which a great deal of the world waited many months for, we had within weeks. The kindness of the Indians who risked their necks with the police to look after us was incredible.

Finally, we heard about Baba beach. Named after a beautiful man who had the keys to the place, this became our hidden paradise, away from the eyes of the police, and began with just a few of us who wanted a place to meditate and to be in the open air. It was too warm in the daytime to be spending it inside rooms with broken fans. At that time, if you were not shopping for essentials, you were immediately questioned or sent home.

We would scurry down the fifteen-minute walk along the side of the Ganga, hoping not to come across the law, our masks shoved in our pockets, and would slip down a side path to find the most pristine and lonely strip of sand among the rocks, away from the streets. It was a tiny paradise, with the views of the mountains all around, and the great Laxman Jhula bridge in the foreground.

I began to teach Gagori's Tai Chi in the mornings on this beach to whomever wanted to learn, desperate to contribute somehow to this beautiful place. It was full of foreigners, and very few Indians; I learnt early on that many Indians are never taught to swim and have a paralysing fear of the water. Some of the men in our group began to teach the locals to swim, and soon there were locals and foreigners creating a new community together.

We would spend blissful mornings as the water got warmer along with the sunshine, bathing and learning to play musical instruments on the sand, drawing intricate rangoli patterns in the wet sand at the water's edge, with no masks on. We became heavily involved in our practices such as pranayama[1], or yoga, exchanging skills from all over the world and talking intelligently about all manner of subjects. It was a dream. For those three hours, we were completely and utterly free.

When we returned on time for curfew back to our hot dwellings, past the police cordons with minutes to spare, we were satisfied and full of joy, for we were experiencing what many would have longed to, across the world. We dutifully did not leave our homes again, happy to have had our morning freedom. With no Covid reported for miles, the village bubble seemed to be working well.

Ninja missions to the hidden restaurants after curfew came with heavy risk attached, but we had to eat, and many of us did not have kitchens. The police checks were frequent and came quickly, and their eagle-eyes spotted anyone who was out of place. Their bamboo sticks terrified us all and we risked fines and being thrown out of our hotels if we were caught. Aidan was reprimanded with an iron pole across the back of the legs, which bruised for weeks, for sitting by the water. I often found myself flat against a wall, hoping their torches would not find me. It was not fair, but it was what we had to do to survive. It gave an element of danger to our lives which made that tiny town a bit livelier in the hot sweaty days to come.

---

1. Pranayama: A series of exercises with the breath which are said to clear physical and emotional obstacles in the body, which releases and harnesses the flow of prana, or life energy.

BABA RAM DASS

I remember the first time I was taken to meet him. His name was Baba Ram Dass, and he was a Sadhu[1] of Rishikesh, who wore only a loin cloth around his waist. This was not the famed Ram Dass, spiritual teacher, and icon of the sixties, but this man did make an excellent cup of chai.

He prepared our tea in an enormous pot over a simple fire made from cow dung, parted on one side to reveal smoking embers which were always alight in his low-ceiling smoke-filled dwelling. He spoke only Hindi, of which at the time I knew very little. It did not matter; Baba Ram Dass had stories he wanted to tell in his native tongue, and I was only too happy to listen to them. It is a strange thing when you are not proficient in a language, but sometimes the connection between two humans is strong enough that the words do not matter: only the intention. It was this way with Baba Ram Dass and me. I nodded in agreement at appropriate times, and kept his steely, one-eyed gaze.

He had one functioning eye; the other was beautiful, white, and cloudy, with a tinge of blue to it. He had thick eyebrows for a man of his age, though I did not dare ask how old he was as my ingrained British etiquette stopped me, thinking it rude, but that did not matter here. It seemed irrelevant, anyway.

He was a Kalpvasis Sadhu, a holy person who had renounced his worldly desires favour of a life dedicated to spiritual practices, staying by the river, to meditate, bathe, and perform Sadhana, or spiritual practices, to attain their spiritual goal.

His hair was white, and in the centre of his eyebrows, or Ajna[2], was a dot of vermillion powder. He was incredibly fit but skinny, abdominal muscles showing through the thin layer of pristine white cloth he had now draped over him to protect him from the cold. As he stirred the pot, he sang. He softly hummed mantras I had never heard and kept holding my hand as if to transfer them to me.

He would not let me help him take the very heavy pot from the embers, and after we had had our fill of chai, he would ask my friends and I to stay awhile just to be in his company. His hut was always open to visitors, and several cushions piled around the edges meant that many people would shelter inside there if the weather turned unfavourable. Little did we know that we would need his shelter more than ever, on many occasions.

A rat casually scratted about in the rafters, and one day, as I drank my chai, it dropped from the ceiling and down the neck of my kurti, and I remember not flinching a bit as it scuttled along my back and scampered off. I decided later that this was confirmation that my nervous system had regulated and calmed and taken on India's relaxed nature. Baba Ram Dass watched the whole encounter, did not bat an eyelid, and simply offered more chai.

Baba Ram Dass was beloved by many westerners, and the

little strip of sand which lay at the bottom of the windy steps that passed by his house was a sanctuary to many of us in India's pandemic lockdown. It was affectionately named 'Baba Beach' by most of us after Baba Ram Dass himself. That little strip of beach was our reason to get up in the morning and was a sliver of sandy hope for us all when social distancing kept us apart in the street, and no gatherings of any kind were allowed. As word spread, almost every foreigner in Rishikesh visited that beach at some point and was allowed safe passage through Baba Ram Dass's gate which joined the street. One day, we woke up to find that they had extended our hours of freedom until afternoon, and the foreigners took every advantage of this time to be in the outdoors. The only rule was no large gatherings. Unfortunately, the popularity of the beach now definitely counted as a gathering.

The police, on their constant patrols, were relentless and ruthless, but Baba Ram Dass had covered his entryway with a cloth so that they could not detect if it was properly fastened or not. Sometimes, in the very early mornings, it would not be open. He would arrive with a smile and often give a pat on the head to those who passed through, and in return for this safe route to our favourite spot we would often bring gifts such as chapatti flour. He never asked for these, though once brought, the responsibility of keeping our friend in chapattis was one that most of us were very willing to bear. The alternative route meant a bit of a climb over the huge rocks that lined the Ganga, or a swim from a nearby Ashram[3], who were becoming suspicious of the early-morning pattering of feet. This place was special, our well-hidden secret, and it was on the minds of no one to accidentally reveal our hiding-place.

Finally, the police arrived in full force. They managed to

47

find Baba Ram Dass's gate unlocked, perhaps due to the care-lessness of an eager foreigner, but the footfall was so high that day that it could have been Baba Ram Dass himself, who had joined us more than once on the beach that morning for a chillum[4] with some of the hippier crowd. As they rounded the corner, an alert was called out, and it all happened rather quickly. Most fled into the water, which was a safe place because the police, in their yellow-beige uniforms, would not venture in.

The problem was that it was cold mountain water, and to stay in there for longer than five minutes was a feat in the March temperatures. Luckily, the sun was on our skin, and we waded and swam over to the nearest exit point, to reach the road. The police were already ahead of us; seeing the direction in which we had so hastily gone, some of us were captured and fined, and some beaten with sticks. This 'bamboo massage', as it was now so frequently and affection-ately known by, was no joke, and left bruises for days on the skin of its victims. Most of them were not bamboo as some of them were walking sticks and the like, fashioned specifi-cally to intimidate those who stepped out of line or missed their curfew by a minute.

The police by this time in the lockdown were low in number in Rishikesh, and so they had quite publicly enlisted the help of some of the locals, who were more than happy to hit the odd foreigner with whatever was at hand. Perhaps this was years of revenge for westerners wearing inappro-priate clothing in their holy town or drinking the odd beer. Perhaps the pandemic and all the fear that came with it, of not being able to protect their beloved town, was driving their hands. Whatever the provocation, they were wonderful with their aim, usually smacking the odd shin and turning it black and blue, but sometimes, an unlucky one would get one to the head. Reporting of this unfairness was rare, especially as quite often the commissioner would go on business elsewhere, leaving his child behind the desk wearing his hat. It was difficult to plead your case to a stamp-happy pre-teen with an ego the size of Mumbai.

Baba Ram Dass stood that day in solemn quiet atop the precipice that overlooked the beach. He was so still and unresponsive, his facial expression blank, a vision of peace and compassion in a moment of such madness. He seemed to be watching over us all. The police did not bother him, and I suppose he feigned ignorance. Later however, it was revealed that he had heard the officers arrive and had scooped up twenty or so of our community and hidden them in his hut just in time to keep them safe. The police on the beach gave up, not suited to the pursuit of sandalled, dreadlocked musicians hastily stuffing half-eaten papayas and well-thumbed copies of 'The Power of Now' into their string bags as they ran.

I heard that he had finally passed on only the other day, more than a year after my Rishikesh experience had ended. Baba Ram Dass will remain one of the most fantastically interesting characters I have had the pleasure of meeting, and I was immensely saddened by his passing. However, in India it is not customary to be sad. I will remember him as a calm, wise storyteller, his very nature admired by so many. After all, Sadhu means 'mild one'. If enlightenment is the individual becoming universal, then Baba Ram Dass was the very image of that.

Two new Sadhus live there now, and when they were asked of his whereabouts, they simply pointed to the sky. Baba Ram Dass, friend to many and guardian of Baba Beach, thank you for the chai.

1. Sadhu: means 'mild one'. Their aim is to become universal, nothing and everything, a holy person with no ties to their human life.
2. Ajna: A chakra point, the 'third eye', a centre of intuition and insight.
3. Ashram: A holy space, where sadhus, yogis and teachers study Sanskrit texts and practice yoga and meditation.
4. Chillum: A clay or wooden smoking pipe, which is filled with hash, opium or charras.

MANGO SEASON

The Sadhus knew first, their pockets stuffed to the brim, fabric sacks tied to sticks to carry them all. They had scoured the feet of the trees where the mangoes grew and picked them clean. Some had camped there for weeks, waiting for them to ripen into perfect yellow-green jewels.

It was Mango Season. We had waited for them to arrive; mouths watering at the thought of them, the whispers that they would soon come laughed from the mouths of babes in bare feet. Plentiful, small, and sweet, the mangoes were piled high on the backs of trucks from the fields by local farmers, a welcome gift to the rising June heat in Rishikesh. The juice-sellers had never been so busy, the markets had never been so frantic, and there were joyful smiles on the faces of everyone in the town. Juice dripping from chins, clothes and fingers stained, the people of Rishikesh sat by the river to have their fill.

The Indian way to enjoy mango in the heat is to place it in the river. It can be steadied between two rocks, or in a fabric bag tied to a stick, and the rushing water then cools the fruit. It is said that the pip holds the heat of the sun. To eat a mango in the Indian way you do not peel the skin away but create a hole in the top and suck out the ripe insides, squeezing out every drop of deliciousness. I lost many a mango to the roaring Ganges, and many a watermelon, for that matter. Mango-drunk, the cows of Rishikesh got the skins, and probably the pips, too, a welcome change from cardboard, burnt chapattis and tinfoil.

There is something about Mangoes and India and a feeling of hope. Just as the desert waits for rain or the first smell of snow comes on the wind as it sprinkles from the sky, just as we wait for the first shoots of Spring, or the coloured leaves to drop in Autumn, India waits for Mango Season.

Joy and hope are not to be taken lightly. The slums in Mumbai flood every year with the Monsoon rains, and families lose every possession they have, and must rebuild, year after year. I have seen street beggars in Delhi with harrowing ailments, disabilities and diseases dying in hedge ways outside towering five-star hotels. I have slept in royal palaces in Rajasthan but held the hands of the gypsy mothers who cannot feed their babies.

Mangoes represent hope, a time of abundance, where the poor can have richness in their pockets, where something that drops from a tree is, for those life-giving, first few weeks, valuable like gold.

INDIAN SUMMER

With the heat came thunderstorms which cracked and sparked all over the valley, with violet skies from dusk until dawn. Great bolts of lightning struck trees in the jungle, the booming of the thunder sounding through the ceiling of every homestay in the town. It was an Indian summer, but it was a wet one, humid and heavy.

As the rains persisted, the monkeys changed their daily course; on more than one occasion a monkey was found in the deepest of slumbers, under the plastic sun chair outside my door, and when woken, bared their teeth against my entry or rather, exit, into the warm bath that was the night air. I gave up wearing underwear after one such creature stole every piece I had, and I would watch in amusement as they tried to steal everything else in the alleyway with their babies clinging to their backs. To leave the door open to catch a rare breeze would have been insanity, as the mere waft of a banana skin in the rubbish bin was enough to entice them in, enormous male specimens with knife-like jaws and muscles on their muscles.

I soon moved; the inability to breathe real air in lockdown was too much to stand, after sometimes eighteen hours in one room.

To move was an endeavour; it took twelve failed attempts visiting various police offices and the peals of laughter from another fifteen-year-old child posing as the chief commissioner in a mud hut before they finally took my passport and threatened to quarantine me if I did move; only tears of anger and frustration saved me.

Move I did, past the police barriers, and near a temple, which played music every evening for Puja, or daily worship, and overlooked the Ganges, for half the price of the soulless hotel I had been stuck in for those few months. This tiny room was basic, with a hard bed, but the balcony was all mine, and the windows on all sides were much needed in the heat. After being hermetically sealed in at night for months, I woke with the morning light.

I found a secret music shop that opened its doors for five minutes per day on the sly and bought a tiny ukulele to pass the time in the evenings. It was perfect timing, as blackouts turned the town to complete darkness and charging electronics was futile. A momo and samosa stand opened at the corner, to serve both the Tibetan and Hindu police who stood by the barrier to the bridge, and underneath my guesthouse, a chai shop lifted its shutters for us to sneak underneath. We sat in the shade and drank ten-rupee sweet milky tea together, locals and foreigners alike. The police got know my face and would allow me to purchase food there. For forty rupees, the steamed vegetable dumplings with chilli sauce, and for ten rupees freshly made potato samosas were a very welcome treat, and light on the pocket. My guesthouse was serving an entire thali for eighty rupees, and a Shiva, or Bael fruit juice which locals said would ward off Covid and stomach aches, which was delicious. The fruit stalls were cheap, and many days I lived on watermelon alone, in the heat of the day. I was very contented and was beginning to see how easy it was to survive in India.

Most of us had given up trying to catch a flight home by this point, as often they were three times the price, and we were living so cheaply that we had all decided to wait it out. I had said goodbye to my Israeli friends months ago, as their military and embassy snapped into action and personally picked up all the foreigners from their doors. Much to my amusement, the English embassy had not contacted me at all, and my airline promised I would get a refund at the end of the pandemic. I was running out of money. Despite the cheap living costs, I had never intended to stay in India for so long, and with the news of my second cancelled repatriation flight home, it looked like I would be staying in India for some time.

Trapped I was, still, but so was everyone else. The camaraderie and humour surrounding it all was always present, especially from our Indian community, who suggested that we marry their brothers and sisters and cousins, so that we could stay with them for longer. One kind local man even offered me a plot of land to build a house, so that we could be neighbours forever.

Desperate for money, I snuck over the bridge to a nearby spa hotel, whose therapist had left due to Covid, and rented a little spa room of my own. My clients would sneak there too, and I was then able to get cash for my efforts, which sustained me for months to come. It was a risk I was willing to take, though it had to be done in the dead of night, or before sunrise.

We missed the evening curfew several times and had to plot a route through the jungle, where elephants and leopards were often reported. I think that most foreigners would have rather taken on leopards than the police at that time, as they were bored, and most of them drank heavily.

The jungle route was the old route into the town, and because of the pandemic, it was now completely deserted apart from the odd farmer, and so I would use it to go jogging. Those early mornings without another single soul were precious, until one morning, mid-jog, I got a funny feeling and slowed my pace. It was then that I heard a large bush growl at me. Knowing better than to investigate, the snarling, raspy and scratchy noise that had come from the undergrowth was a sound unlike anything I have heard in my life.

I turned on my heel and sprinted in the opposite direction, laughing as I got a stitch and could finally stop, shaking in fear and the realisation that I could have easily made a fantastic breakfast for some beast. As I got home, I Googled the noise of a leopard, and the sound I had heard was confirmed to me; I had probably had a very lucky escape. I did not go back that way for some time, at least not alone.

"Don't Google. Google is inside you." – *Gagori*

MONSOON PETS

I lay beside threadbare windowpanes and poorly measured mosquito netting, which let in every drop of rain. Temperatures had soared in the week that had passed, and as I lay bare atop questionable sheets and pillows soaked in mould, on the hardest bed in my India experience, I was grateful for the rain drops.

A priority in the mornings became watching the washing; the merest hint of rain could turn to a downpour in seconds, and would last all day, so nothing whatsoever was drying. At night, power cuts plagued the town, and reading by candlelight became my only solace. The air was completely still, thick, and steamy. Even the shower gave up, spitting tiny dribbles of brown water every few days the temperature of the sun. I ate only watermelon, and, unable to keep my own heat down, I fasted and stopped moving very far at all, only to venture to the river or the chai wallah underneath my residence.

Even the river Ganga was going through changes; she had turned a mucky brown, and the bank of my home, which included several ashrams and temples, was a perfect spot to sit and watch her sucking and churning. The power that she had was shocking and sometimes she would erupt with no warning, from the middle, water spraying up for metres directly into the air. The locals told me that she was digesting, thinking, and transitioning, cleansing herself of all the negative energy, and I thought how beautiful that explanation was; the river was considered a Goddess, and they gave her time to renew and heal, where no one dared to swim in her wrath. India has a strong connection to the feminine, and none more so than their river Ganga. If there was a model for me to follow in terms of renewal, she was it, in a constant state of perpetual clearing.

I began to bathe in the Ganga like the locals. At night, it became customary to put on long clothes to cover your body and lie floating in the water as enormous bats flew overhead and the smell of opening jasmine flowers floated down the ghats. Afterwards, we each collected a bucket of cold Ganga water to take to bed. I lay on my mattress in soaking wet clothes trying to sleep, and when it became unbearable, I would throw both my hands into the bucket beside me, and dunk my feet, or again wet my clothes, for a few minutes of relief until they too, dried in the instant heat.

Sleep eventually came, but so did the beasts. Snakes wrestled to the death in the water where we bathed, and rats hurried over the banks. One night a poisonous black millipede crawled from between the slats of my bed. Hunting it was futile, as the power went out once more, and it was never found.

The Huntsman spiders were the size of lampshades, and they had thick bristly legs and jumped from wall to wall. I would lie there and reason with them, asking only for them not to drop on me in the night, and they seemed to take notice. Finally came the cockroaches. I eradicated cardboard from my room after the startling discovery of a family of roaches living in boxes of teabags. Various creatures ran amok on the floors at night, and my little bottle of peppermint oil was not enough to deter them. These temporary Monsoon insects were growing in number, despite the strength of my essential oils being daubed around the place.

Just as we had all learnt to live together in relative harmony, I stepped on something at four o'clock in the morning and it burst under my foot. I screamed, and my neighbour tapped on my door in concern. It turned out that, despite my best efforts to ward off the wildlife, he had been cooking on the floor of his room, and as we opened his door multiple cockroaches fled, scuttling between the pots and pans. They raced across the hall and immediately squeezed under the crack in my door. The next morning, I went to look for somewhere else to sleep.

In the next few months to come, I learned how to welcome her in, the primal, wild woman I had somehow lost along the way. I discarded my shoes, hardening the soles of my feet. I grew out the hair on my legs. I meditated daily at sunrise and sunset and learnt how the moon affected my mood. I climbed trees. I turned my attention inwards, spending whole days in silence, refusing to speak at all. I ate when I was hungry and fasted when I was not. I spent long nights with a Brazilian and an Israeli man who called me Devi, or Godess, allowing myself to dissolve into sweet surrender, who held me in their strong arms. I lay down to watch the stars at night and wondered how I had never found the time to.

I needed less, wanted less, expected less, and found more. I felt as if every part of me was changing, evolving, learning; revolving around a wheel which would eventually click into place and hold me there. I no longer noticed my hard mattress, my mouldy ceiling, or my cold shower.

It was a clearing. A clearing of my own path, a getting out

of my own way. I was trying to rid myself of all that felt unnecessary, that which I was clinging on to and was holding me back from finding calm. I penned long lists of my mistakes and burnt them under the full moon, or threw them to the Ganga, to be swallowed by her swirling waters. I forgave others for how they had wronged me, became bored of the stories I told myself and forgave myself for the anger I had carried, letting it go. I started to ask myself what I wanted in life and started to walk away from what I did not. I learnt the word no and how to use it, and finally I came back to myself lighter and more alive. With the distance, I noticed how I was able to question many things about my homeland and my experience on a small island. It occurred to me that perhaps I had outgrown it some time ago and that I was looking for answers that England could not give me.

India was shaping me in every way, though I did not know. Often, like the body work Gagori had taught me, we cannot see such tiny adjustments, until suddenly your crippling pain is gone, and you are standing straighter than before.

"How long have you been here? Yes, In India. Yes, you!
Do not stay too long here; you will never survive back home."
- Chaiwallah, Rishikesh

GAGORI'S NEXT LESSON

One evening, after Aarti, I met a man on the side of the ghat leading down to Ganga. He was making music with sound bowls and asked me to join him. He taught me the technique so that the sound rang smoothly, a relaxed hand, a slow pace, a steady resonating bowl at my feet. It was very beautiful. I got up to leave and thanked him for the new skill, and he stared at me very intensely for a moment. He motioned for me to sit again, and told me,

"Do not get involved in the business of the universe. It is not your business."

This both scared and annoyed me. This man did not know me, and it sounded about as judgmental as anything I'd ever heard.

"What we don't like in others reflects what we do not like in ourselves. They are a good mirror and can help us." – Gagori

The next night, I heard a kitten mewling for its mother.

The sound was piteous, and it cut through to the core of me, like I imagine the sound of a baby crying does for new mothers. I went to investigate.

"Let's comfort it," I said, to my friend, with whom I was sat. The kitten was on a high wall. We stroked it for a bit, and it continued crying. I walked away, unable to bear the noise of its sobs as I was feeling low that week, my beloved cat having died back in the UK. The next thing I knew, the kitten had been plonked in my arms as we sat on the ghats.

"To cheer you up," my mate said.

We knew all the street dogs, and they trusted us. We sat with a tiny kitten in our arms, and they did not stir, did not sniff at her. Now, at this time, I was attending some workshops to do some therapy and realised that many of my problems stemmed from control; of others, and of many things in life that I could not change. Someone next to me asked the hold the kitten, and it was through this self-work that I decided to trust; I closed my eyes and breathed through the anxiety I felt at giving up control of this small thing in my arms, knowing others were also capable of taking care of something. Little did I know that this was my intuition shouting, for I opened my eyes to see the kitten taking steps down the ghat; the girl to whom I had entrusted the kitten had become distracted.

What happened next was so quick that I had to strain my eyes to see, but one street dog, my favourite companion whom I had sat with at every sunset, snapped her up in his jaws and broke the kitten's neck. She hung from his mouth, struggling. My friend gave chase and caught the street dog, and as we wrestled the tiny baby from his mouth, and saw the foam at her lips, all we could do was hold this tiny thing and wait for the end. We sang mantras as she took her last breath, and slipped her quietly into the Ganga, apologising over and over in whispered shame.

Walking home, I had a panic attack from the guilt and sat on the pavement to breathe or try to. My favourite cow walked up to me and stood face to face, pushing her head to my forehead. I stayed like that for a long time, holding onto her neck, feeling her grounded presence. She did not move for maybe twenty minutes as I cried heavy tears down her nose. I wonder to this day if she felt my pain, too.

By getting involved in something that was not my business, as the strange man had foretold or foreseen, we had directly contributed to the killing of that innocent kitten. I could not bear to lie with the dogs on the steps at sunset any longer, blaming them out of shame. I could not look at the girl who let the kitten out of her arms. This was not helping anyone; I forgave them, and then after some time, eventually forgave myself.

I realised two things that day. One; that my intuition is the strongest thing I know, and that my power is in listening to it. Two, that when Mama India wants to teach you a lesson, she will choose something that will stay with you forever.

DENGUE, CORONA, RABIES, OR MALARIA

It is considered a souvenir of India to leave with a motorbike exhaust pipe burn or a monkey scratch. As it would turn out, I would leave with both, but on this occasion, an experience with the latter left me very sick indeed.

As I was sneaking illegally across Laxman Jhula bridge one morning, as I was accustomed to doing so at this time, because I was living and working on opposite sides, I saw a troop of monkeys at the other end of the bridge. I told myself that this was the time to get over my fear.

The usual chant of "No monkeys, no monkeys, no monkeys," though it had often worked so many times before, had not worked for me this day, and there they were, the protectors of the bridge.

I steadied my breathing and did what I knew to do, avoiding eye contact, protecting my neck, and tucking in loose clothing that could be viewed as a toy. I breathed out through the whole troop, though they were inches from my ankles and my shoulders at all levels like a gang, swinging from the suspension poles on the bridge, over the gateway, and swiping at me from the floor. One particularly aggressive male swiped a little too close to me as I leapt to safety, past the railings, and he caught my arm. Rabies playing on my mind, I went to the police, who sniggered and said that this male monkey was known to them to be dangerous, and that I should make haste right away, to the local mini hospital down the road.

The hospital consisted of four chairs which had possibly been taken from a public bus, and situated outside, in the heat. The walls were plastered haphazardly with Covid posters in Hindi, covering the mould. The consultation cost twenty rupees, and the receptionist tried immediately to give me a packet of broad-spectrum antibiotics, without any diagnosis at all.

"*Namaste ji, kya aap angrezee, bolate hai?*" I said, as politely as I could, asking him if he spoke English.

"Nahin, Ma'am. Hindi," he replied, shaking his head and gesturing to the chairs outside.

I gestured to my arm and did an impression of a monkey. Mild interest crossed his face for a second before he returned to his phone. When my turn came, I was shouted at from the back room. A man in jeans and a t-shirt casually indicated to the hospital bed, and immediately tried to sink a needle into my arm.

"Ji," I protested, "You must flick the needle! For bubbles! Look!" I showed him. He shrugged and flicked it a bit. I swallowed my panic and watched him; he had absolutely no idea what he was doing. We were not done; he motioned to the bed and made me lie down flat. I hesitated; the door was open and the whole waiting room was watching, and he wanted me to reveal my bum cheek. I did so, laughing, and again shrieked as he did not flick the needle. I sat up in disbelief and explained,

"Sir, this is for safety!" He dutifully flicked it several times and let some fluid escape from the top, and I turned over to finally let him administer the drug.

Some hours later, I began to feel very poorly. As if in preparation for some disaster to strike, I collected a few essential items from the shops; bottled water in a five-litre, though my arm was now a swinging dead weight by my side, and some crackers. I thought it might last me the night. Three days later, I was aware that days and nights had passed. I woke up and had completely overturned my bed; the hallucinations and the heat had driven me to sleep in the shower, and my whole body was a shivering mess.

I am unsure as to how high my temperature had risen. I was not hungry but knew I should drink; the water was still untouched. I received flashbacks of the last few days in my room, of the visions. I saw a huge snake crawling from the light switch and staring me in the eyes, leaving me frozen in fear. I went on a never-ending search for the black millipede that lived under the bed, destroying my room in the process.

I finally dressed in some random piece of fabric and staggered to the nearby restaurant, my nearest safe house, where the boys from the balcony knew me well enough. Their reaction to my pallid and sweating appearance told me all I needed to know; and to their credit they did not immediately label me with Coronavirus but walked me back to my guesthouse with a bowl of Khichdi, which they claimed could cure everything. I ate a few spoonfuls and slept, the fever rising once more, and every time I awoke to eat, the cardamom in the bowl turned to beetles stuck between my teeth. I felt them in my mouth as they crawled away, over my lips, down the spoon, and back into the bowl. I did not eat the rest, unable to decipher in my delirious state if this was real or imagined.

I called a friend, who dropped off bananas at the door and water, the threat of Coronavirus palpable. I managed neither.

At some point and I do not know when, I managed to wander down through the streets, dishevelled and clutching only my passport and five hundred rupees. I walked to the nearest place that offered air conditioning, determined to reduce the fever. To my surprise, they let me in with kindness, ignoring the strict rules of the police, and turned on the air conditioning. I slept. The next morning, I woke up frozen, but my fever had finally passed.

To my mind, it was either the Rabies vaccination, Covid, Dengue or Malaria, but I will never know. After offering once again some broad-spectrum antibiotics, the doctors gave me some serious-looking fever pills and confirmed, on a piece of paper, that I had nothing wrong with me, and that anyhow, I had waited far too long to be tested. He told me to keep wearing my mask and to stay far away from bananas. I accepted that, for twenty rupees, I couldn't ask for any more.

NIRVANA

The heat of the Monsoon had affected us all, and we were all desperate for an escape and for cold water as Ma Ganga was still deliberating, her colour now as black as Kali's skin, Goddess of Destruction. Luckily, I was now sheltering in one of the only rooms in the town with air conditioning, which came and went, but gave some momentary relief between power cuts. It had red strip lighting in the ceiling and thick blackout curtains and was a damp, seedy-looking place with no windows. It was a strange kind of existence, with the rains coming thick and fast every day, and sometimes I did not see sunlight at all due to the closeness of the houses and the black of the sky. Every piece of my clothing was wet and would not dry.

Someone had the bright idea to hire a campsite outside of our little town and made a festival. People came from all over to share their gifts and the days were spent teaching and learning from each other with people from all over the world, in this tiny space in the mountains. It was just what everyone needed.

In the heat, we threw ourselves into the freezing river,

one of the tributaries that joined the rushing Ganges in Rishikesh. It ran clear, like the Ganga had before Monsoon, and was so inviting. I was surprised to see that almost everyone immediately took off their clothes; naked bodies holding hands in the stream and diving from rocks, cuddling amongst the banks. I sat there in my modest swimwear in awe. The resistance I felt was extraordinary.

How, in all that I had learnt so far, was I still so shy and unyielding?

I watched a girl throw her head back and laugh, striding among the pebbles, she looked like a warrior, a queen. I longed to be her, I wished for that easy confidence, that natural easy way of being, where she did not have to think twice about showing herself to the world. I felt my English conditioning rise in me, to cover myself, to protest somehow, not knowing where these feelings came from. I was desperate to join them all; I did not know how.

I remembered my mother, her breasts exposed every summer to catch the sun's rays, and the embarrassment I had felt sometimes at that simple act; she had been a wonderful role model in this way, but I had never understood back then, I was too full of insecurity. This judgement of myself was readily programmed in, and I did not know when it started, only that I wanted to rid myself of it.

The sun went down, and I sat with two male friends under the full moon. We looked at each other and grinned; now was the time. Alone in the dark, we threw off all our clothes and our bodies sparkled under the moonlight, white and glistening as the cold water hit us all. I shook it all off and howled to the night sky.

I remembered the day I had stood bare in front of my massage group. Their eyes saw only a vehicle, an assessment, a scientific example.

If the body was a vehicle, then why did so many of us attach such negativity to it?

The strength that it had taken to discard my clothes on the massage table some months ago was playing on my mind, and the next day, I was the first one into that river.

I strode across the pebbles myself, waving to the girl who had inspired me, Mia, a French woman who might have been the most feminine spirit I have ever met, and we smiled at each other across the rippling water. The water moved like her, her body and the liquid ripples were one. I remember thinking that she was perfect. I know now that we all were.

That night, I danced in ecstasy around a fire with my tribe. I felt like I was shining like that river that had washed away every trace of my shame and left only confidence. With every snaking movement to the deep bass, I ground my past self into the floor with warrior steps and thought of the Indian Goddess Kali, as I stuck out my tongue and beat my hands to my chest, wild and free, and raw. If Kali is the embodiment of 'Shakti', or 'female' energy, then I invoked the feminine that night. Like I had been wearing heavy shackles, a weight was lifted from somewhere in my body as I danced under the pearly moon.

It would take a whole community of incredible characters in India to slowly reveal sides of me I never knew. I owe my life to those people who showed me their authentic selves and became my mirrors, teaching me important lessons. They are all my gurus.

FALLING IN LOVE IN INDIA

To be in India with a lover is to see India through two pairs of eyes, but they are rose-tinted, and all of India is more so awash with beauty than ever before. Every journey is a chance to look up from a book and catch a shy smile, every morning is lustful and sleepy-eyed, and every cold night is a warm comforting embrace.

My lovers' eyes were a periwinkle blue that matched his shirts if he ever wore clothes. He was a wild animal of a man; a strong, confident, intelligent South African with a sweet nature and a penchant for risky behaviour. Anywhere that he wanted to be, I was adamant that I would stay. We had fallen in love with each other's minds before our bodies and hearts did, so quickly and completely that we had never looked back, never coming out of the honeymoon period. Our relationship developed into something that, I think, scared us both witless.

John was a writer, and we met at a poetry reading, on a fairy-lit rooftop in Rishikesh, in October. He told a story about a dog and a train, and it was not the tale itself that reeled me in, but his voice and intention; as if commanding the attention of a room was too juicy for him, as if he was savouring each word he was saying, feeling it resonate out into the space, knowing that he was captivating. He was off script and engaging, and I remember thinking,

Who is this man, and why is he so charming?

As I told my own story about an old Indian city, I did not see him in the crowd, and did not know if he was watching. When I got up to leave, he came to find me and told me my words had resonated with him deeply. It must have been the universe bashing me hard on the head as I lifted him down to the end of the lane, a tiny three-minute drive on a scooter that turned out to be the best decision I would make in a long time, my cheeks red and his smile shining. He came to my birthday party, and our hands met over gathered fire-wood and eyes shone across the spitting flames. When he kissed my cheek goodbye, I knew it was not for the last time.

Coffee came next, the date that was not a date, but that was, and then it was all over, because I fell in love, with his sparkling wit before his hard body, John grabbing my neck and holding me tight as his tongue interlaced with mine. We kissed by the statue of Shiva[1], and I laughed as he said that Shiva probably wouldn't mind.

I came in for a cup of tea, which we knew wasn't tea at all but would be the end of everything, would be sparkling conversation, lips on collarbones and the breaking of furniture that would lead to an all-consuming connection. I was sure that this connection would burn for the rest of my life.

---

1. Shiva: The creator, destroyer and restorer of the Universe in Hinduism, he represents both good and evil.

MORNING ROUTINES

Wearing your favourite shirt, I gaze at you, tea towel draped over one shoulder. You feed me concoctions, potions from your kitchen, and I make the bed. Bare-bottomed, we pour strong coffee into mismatched mugs with smashed handles.

You wash my feet, lathering soap, and dry each toe with careful caresses, on your knees on the cold, hard floor. I take the towel and I too, in turn, bend to one knee to clean your feet. I watch you with interest; it is a curious thing, this equal pairing. You carry me to bed; strong arms hold me tightly and I let you.

As we make love, you cry into my chest. We try to place our role in this space, in wonder, for this is not like the others. This is unmarked territory, and the ground is new soil. To stamp here would kick up dust, but I do not feel like stamping. I want to roll in it, dig it up deep, and make rivets, plant seeds and water this land, the garden of us, and watch it struggle and thrive into life.

MATA JI

Mata Ji, which means respected mother, was the most foul-tempered old woman I have met in possibly all of India. I encountered her on the road on my daily walk, in the heat of the morning, as she fanned herself with a paper plate. She lay dramatically as if fallen, draped over a partition of a wall outside the local bakery, dressed in brightly coloured, ill-fitting clothes, which revealed the skinniest arms I have ever witnessed on anyone still living. Her hair was cropped short, grey hair shining against deeply brown crepe-paper skin. Her mouth turned up at the edges as if she was always keeping in a smile, which quickly turned sour at all manner of things happening in the street. It was always a fun game to see which one she would greet you with.

She would ask for two chapatis from everyone who passed. At first, I would nod and ignore her, as many westerners had been taught to do to the many beggars around India. However, it did not feel right to do so. There was energy about her that I cannot explain, and the first time that I next passed her, I had forgotten money and instead just shared my banana with her. Her face lit up in genuine grate-fulness, and I told myself I would never ignore her again. I brought her bananas most days after that, and she would smile as I kept one of the bunches for myself, gave a few to her, and one to the local cow who also frequented that spot.

I did get her those two chapatis after all. She was delighted that her request had been acknowledged and she put it in her bag. I wondered how many people had gone to the trouble. I realised quite quickly that she did not have the stamina for walking, and when I witnessed a local taking her by the arm to walk down the hill, I saw first-hand just how frail she was.

One day, she was wearing bandages on her arm. I asked her what happened, and she replied with a perfect snarl and a monkey gesture, that one had bitten her. I quickly tele-phoned my friend who was giving first aid to the Sadhus as his form of service during the lockdown; he was aware of her plight and was in the chemist to procure antibiotics for her.

I imagined her defending herself from the colossal monkeys that inhabited Rishikesh. I knew that she had a stick, but after facing some hefty monkeys the week before-hand and having to surrender my groceries, I knew that it was a tough situation for an elderly woman such as herself to overcome. Bananas suddenly did not seem enough of a gesture on my part, but soon enough, she was off the streets and away from my watchful gaze, as she succumbed to sickness.

Mata Ji passed on, I am told, at the grand age of one hundred and eight, but in India that number is so auspicious that she may well have been eighty-five for all the specula-tion around her actual lifespan. I am comforted in the knowledge that occasionally, I made her smile, and if I ever pass the end of her road again, I will leave bananas and two chapatis.

"When we are born, our palms are closed tightly. We do not yet have anything to offer this world. But when we die, our palms are so open. We have given all that we have."
– A Pandit, a Hindu priest, Varanasi

LEARNING TO FLY

The little spark of bravery that began all my biggest adventures could only ever have been born in a place such as India which was chaos and mess, where rules were bent and broken. It started in steps, as one cannot just buy a motorbike with no driving license and hope to drive it out of the shop without any idea of how to even start one up. It started at the end of the first lockdown, as there were whisperings in the air of a second locking down of Uttarakhand.

As much as Rishikesh had been my home, my bubble of safety and my sanctuary, I felt the call. I felt it in my gut, where all the best and worst feelings originate, those which if they are not acted upon, quickly begin to churn like a poisonous soup. This soup was spiky and raw, and it scared me silly, but my mind and my stomach were instantaneously connected in a single thought, which was to hire a motorbike and get out of Rishikesh. I never believed that I had the courage to ride a motorcycle. I always thought motorbikes were for the people with danger written in their stars, rockers, and those sorts of effortlessly attractive people who never seemed to struggle at anything. I thought motorbikes were for rebels, James Dean types, Hollywood starlets in leather jackets putting their lipstick on in the mirror, arms linked around their lovers, or those having a midlife crisis wanting to experience some risk.

I didn't know any female bikers, so I had no role models to speak of, no one to show me that women and biking were a truly magnificent combination, and no one to tell me that I could ride one.

I had no riders in my family, and I had never learnt to drive a car, never mind a motorcycle, and when I told my family what I wanted to do, they laughed, and told me that I was a non-driver, that I was a danger to those on the road. I knew better.

I had gotten quite daring on my rented scooter, which I had taken to immediately despite having never driven one before, and it thrilled me to ride it at speed and through congested traffic and even through the lashing rain, sharpening my immature driving skills and every dangerous bone in my body until I was this fearless, hardened version of myself. Driving in Indian traffic is something many people will never experience, but I would recommend it at least once.

If it were not for a truly adventurous friend, I would probably not have gone alone, even though I said that I would at the time. Looking back, I'd like to believe that I would have persevered, but the very first stumble was my license. I had never had one back in the UK, and was currently driving the scooter illegally, as no one had ever checked. Of course, this was common practice in India, as many Indian people did not have a license at all. If the police caught you, they would usually ask for a hundred rupees, and send you on your way.

My first driving lessons had consisted of teaching myself, driving my mother's 4x4 down our straight but long dirt track at the farm where we lived, and the instances where the young labourer would allow me to man the tractor as he sat in the back and smoked. I even remember being allowed behind the controls of a combine harvester one summer, but I would have never considered myself to be a natural driver.

Matteo, my Rishikesh friend, was game for anything, and when I had suggested an adventure, he had, like me, jumped at the idea of escaping our lockdown home. He had years of experience driving, but never motorcycles. The issue was still that I did not have a legal license, but we had a plan.

He used his own driving licence at two different rental shops and was able to wobble one Royal Enfield 350 out into the nearest car park, where we both spent a few hours doing figure of eights on it until we felt steady enough to drive past the seller again, to appear accomplished. A Royal Enfield is also fondly known as a Bullet, made in the UK or Chennai, and is the oldest global motorcycle brand still in production.

The locals had told tales of two insane people throwing an Enfield around near the chai shop, and the boss had come down to show us a thing or two, or perhaps just for entertainment. In India, most people would rather help you than hinder you. India had a natural culture of helping others, called 'Karma' found within Buddhism, Hinduism and Jainism, a universal law where good actions determine your future existence. For all the challenges India brought us, there was always an undercurrent of goodness.

They wanted to see us ride. Had they come earlier, they would have seen me drop the bike on its side or witnessed my appalling emergency stop. However, after an hour of practicing something which resembled circles, I was more than up for this challenge and flew past them, long blonde hair flying in the wind. They shuffled off, satisfied, and my friend and I beamed at each other.

It was on. We arranged a Bajaj Avenger for me, a cruiser

220cc motorbike which was a bit cheaper to rent, and lower in height. I could get my feet flat on the floor unlike with the Enfield. This first foray into motorbike riding would empower me and finally label something which I had tried to hide for so long, my dominant masculine side.

ODE TO INDIAN ROADS

Don't hesitate, stay in the middle. Pretend you're a man.
Use your horn, as often and as obnoxiously as you can.
Don't be chivalrous, mind your business, overtaking on corners,
yes, I'm serious.
Potholes! Look out; they are metres wide, and deep,
and there are razor-sharp wires ready to catch your feet.
There are nails overturned outside garage bays, and splinters of
wood flying straight at your face.
There are long hanging wires, trailing from a boot, and a welder is
sending sparks into your view.
In the back of vans, there are sharp, pointed skewers,
for the building of houses, but never secured.
Stay far behind the trucks, who are known to brake,
their emergency stops more efficient than yours anyway.
Buses don't see you, try not to die, every few hundred kilometres,
stop for a chai.
Remember which towns have mechanics, and which do not.
Taillights don't matter; people don't indicate, they just stop. Prepare
for backwards-coming cars doing U-turns down motorways.
It's risky, putting your life in the hands of Indian roadways.

THE CLOSE CALL

Before I set off on my motorcycle trip around Uttarakhand, I was haunted in the night by nightmares of hanging white cliff faces. In my dreams, I flew over the edge and felt the drop in my stomach, in my bones. I would startle awake, with severe nerves about what I was about to do, to set off on a trip as a novice rider on a bike I had learnt to ride three days ago. What I did not know was that I would see the very cliff that was in my nightmares, and it would appear to me after one of the most terrifying experiences of my life.

There have been many difficult moments throughout my biking adventures in India. What I have learnt is that it does not matter how well one drives, but how badly everyone else does. In India, there is no highway code to speak of. People will think nothing of driving up the centre of the road going the opposite way, driving in cities without mirrors, without indicating and without hand signals, careering into your path at the speed of light without a second's warning. In India, the only communication comes from your horn.

A horn means "move," or simply, "I'm here." It is custom to beep the horn as you are about to overtake anyone, or as you do anything at any stage, and it is essential to use liberally on narrow mountain passes on every single corner as those roads do not allow for two vehicles.

The rules are very simple: don't get in the way and always exude confidence. There's that belief that nervous drivers are the most dangerous drivers on the road; in India, it would be fatal to hesitate at all. The most tiresome and extremely dangerous move that seems to be a prerequisite to passing your driving test in India is the ability to overtake on a blind corner. As I watched vehicles in front of me attempt it, I sucked air through my teeth and held my breath as cars squeezed into spaces with seconds to spare, their kids in the back seat unbelted, my heart a beating drum of terror, until the next attempt.

Many of the risk takers were the white Maruti Suzuki 800's, low to the ground, so completely impractical for the mountain roads and yet frustratingly the vehicle of choice for many. These small cars irritated me beyond measure. They were prone to breakdowns and often had smoke pouring from exhaust pipes due to the strain of the mountain passes. Their low speed was not helpful; to be stuck behind these for many kilometres became common, the incompetency of the drivers seemingly correlating to the inadequateness of the vehicles.

Most of my near misses came from trucks and these blind corners. Solid and stuck in their ways, Indian trucks do not care for, nor do they see motorbikes and will force you to slip onto the gravelly inner bank to nip past them. Not only is this incredibly dangerous when meeting a truck at high speed, but those lipped edges are uneven and hide all manner of bike hazards: from broken glass, rags of fabric, to sand and thin stones, making you skid out entirely if you're not approaching in first gear. However, with the only other option being steep banks and sheer drops, it is much safer to face a truck's grill than the edge. After this first trip, I vowed never again to be pushed around on the road, choosing instead to slow down and face these trucks head on, laying on the horn and playing chicken or stopping dead until they moved an inch or so for me to pass. I still grumble to anyone who will listen that those who drive should first be made to try a motorbike.

On the day of my accident, we were in a rush. In India, even walking the street too quickly will ensure a passing catcall of "Aram-se, Didi."

Slow down, sister.

Indians attribute rushing to not being at peace with themselves, and this was another lesson I had not yet learnt. It was true; to move slowly and with purpose is to be present and conscious of your surroundings. It is when we are not present that accidents often occur.

If you were to constantly sprain your ankle on the same side, it is said that either your masculine or feminine side is out of balance and is alerting you to this weakness. Walking barefoot works slows you down a great deal, focusing you to be conscious of where you place each foot, each step a choice. Gradually, you slow in every way, your body no longer feeling the need for speed in everything it does. It is the same with the road; just because the option to speed or squeeze in ahead of someone was there, does not mean that I had to take that action. To reach a place of complete calm while driving, regardless of others, is a skill which took me a long time to obtain.

It was a few hours until sunset and as usual, Google maps in its infinite wisdom had guided us many hours short of our target, not accounting for the high inclines. Everyone was trying to get home to their families for their evening meal. The energy on the road was risky and unrelenting, high-speed cars and bikes without lights on hairpin bends as the light faded on every overhanging cliff face. Knowing what I know now, I would have pulled over and sat still for a bit and stayed out of the madness. As it was, we pushed on and India would shout again, loudly, "Aram-se."

Slow down.

A truck pulled in front of my bike just before a hard bend, swiftly and without a horn. In the open back were some rusty steel support rods, which are used for building houses. Normally, these trucks are full to the brim, but this one had fewer, and they were rattling around in the back. In India, trucks may have these sticking out for metres behind them, with nothing to secure them or keep them from falling out. I was always terrified of them, and I believe to this day that the universe was giving me this subtle subconscious fear to keep me from getting too close.

The truck hit the brakes hard, as it spotted another vehicle coming for it face to face, on the wrong side of the road. The overtaking had come at exactly the wrong moment, and everything happened in a split-second. As the truck's brakes slammed on, there was no distance between me and this truck, as it had overtaken me so swiftly. There was no time to stop, and the steel rods were inches from me, headed straight over the top of the bike and into my torso.

I cannot explain how my body knew what to do, but instead of pressing both brakes, my brain chose only the right, which caused my back wheel to lock and my bike to slide, and it pushed me to the side, away from the deadly spikes. It was so close that the spikes caught my bike jacket, which was open, and I believe that if it were not for that jacket, and that split-second decision, I would have been impaled.

I drove recklessly into the other side of the road; the drop on my left was thousands of feet deep. Dumping the bike where I skidded would have meant being run over from behind. I had no other choice, and crossed into the other lane, just clipping an oncoming scooter on the opposite side of the road with two men riding it. I looked back guiltily as they tumbled off and I threw myself to the side as I crashed into the side of the mountain. I turned off the kill switch and lifted the motorcycle from the ground; not a scratch on the paintwork, but the clutch handle was snapped in half where it had skidded. I had walked away without a scratch, save for a tell-tale scrape on my jacket from those deadly steel rods, and with the distinct feeling that I was the luckiest person on the planet.

In India it is custom to offer money to someone you've met in an accident. The men were initially furious, but when they saw the truck and the poles, it explained everything without me having to break out Google Translate. Annoyed but vilified, they sped off, as I tried hastily to stuff money, bandages and first aid ointment into their angry hands and pockets.

When they had left, I sat for a moment on the side of the road with my friend, who had watched it all happen from behind and was also in shock. I swung my leg over my rental bike immediately; my first lesson in horse-riding on the farm was to get straight back on, or risk losing all confidence. I was shaking like a leaf, and probably could have done with a big shot of whisky, but somehow, I got back on the bike.

The cliff came as we rounded a bend, and I had to stop the bike in shock. It was as I had seen it in my dreams, the white cliff unlike any other amongst the brown landscape, the sheer drop with no railing, the curve of the mountain, and even the scattered stones at my feet. I have dreamed several dreams like this in my life, where it felt like a premonition or that I have been somewhere before. As I stared at the gap it seemed to me that I could almost make out tyre tracks, energy stranded there from the reality that could have been. I realised with the same lurch in my stomach, as I relived my recurring dream, that this could have been a very real scenario. The white cliff was precisely what had kept me safe for my whole journey, kept my speed down and my wits sharp on every winding turn.

That white cliff continued to haunt my dreams for the remainder of my trip, but I have never been so grateful for such a ghost.

FEMININITY

I needed to fix the Avenger. Gripping my broken clutch handle with one finger, we rode slowly and carefully until we found a roadside mechanic. He was about seventeen years old, but he was fast and diligent. After he had patched her up again, he asked for a lift to the whisky shop on the back of the bike, to which I obliged.

As we were nearing the shop, his hands snuck round to cup my breast and to stroke my inner thigh as he pretended to hold on, and he wriggled and laughed when he was caught. I remember thinking,

How will he learn unless someone gives him a short, sharp shock?

I stopped the bike and hit him in the chest, hard.

"*Nahin, bhai,*" I said, angrily shaking my head. No, brother.

He dismounted, and I felt dizzy with rage. I pulled out an apple from my pack; I had not eaten in hours, and we had a long journey ahead. I threw one to Matt, on the bike behind me. When the young mechanic asked for one too, I threw it at his head, and told him,

"Chalo jao," Go away.

Had I known more Hindi at this point or had he known any English, I would have tried to educate him. India is not the only country with a lot to learn about how to treat women, for many reasons which mainly point to education. Contrastingly, women and femininity are also hugely celebrated all over India, but many men are still educated only by porn. I could not change the world by reprimanding one teenager, but neither did I have to laugh it off. His hands would not easily be forgotten.

If men knew how the fear of assault was wound so tightly into our very being, they would know that when we cry when someone feels us up in a club, it is the tears of many years of being told our skirts are too short for men to ignore, of being grabbed against our will, or that if we wear red lipstick, we are "asking for it." Riding a motorbike may have given me all the confidence in the world, but for those few seconds of unwarranted touch, I felt as if I had no power at all.

Women's collective stories of defence would wrap the world in a blanket of paper shame if they were all written out in ink. Now I understood the risk of travelling alone, and why many women just preferred to stay at home.

It has been said that modern women are emasculating men. This could be so; many of us have had to rely on our masculine tendencies for so long, to stay safe. Be confident, argue back, show no fear. Yet we are also expected to be more feminine, be softer, cool our tempers, be nicer.

I remembered my eighteen-year-old self, walking home alone from night shifts in London. I tied my hair back so that I could hear footsteps behind me, placed house keys in between my fingers, and wore flat shoes, ready to run. My senses were already sharp and refined even then. For most of history, women's nervous systems have been in a perpetual state of alert, and I thought about how unfair that was. Travelling alone had meant mine were heightened further still.

I thought about what 'being feminine' truly meant. I thought about the Goddess Kali, and how India celebrates her, her image depicted as wild, her tongue lolling from her mouth, standing on her lover as he submits to her. Anger is also inherently a feminine trait, even if we have been told that it is not, and that, "nice girls smile."

*"Make two cups of tea. One for your anger, and one for you." -
Gagori*

I thought about how many definitions of femininity also reflect softness, love, and compassion, and as I looked at his torn and dirty clothes, unwashed hair, I also remembered the blanket on the floor in his little hut on the freezing mountain. I looked at the bottle of cheap whisky in his hand, I saw his embarrassed face, and suddenly he looked so small. I believe that the shock of being dealt with in such a way by a female westerner was more than enough to shame the boy because I saw the guilt in his eyes. He would remember this day, as we all remember our shame.

I threw him one more disapproving look and drove away, and a few minutes later as I followed Matt's taillights in the darkness, I hung back and yelled until my lungs burned. Directing my anger to the skies felt like a good compromise; I was learning not to swallow my emotion, but neither would I let them consume me. Like Gagori said, I would make my anger a cup of tea.

CONNECTION

Some devotees sit their whole lives. There are stories of those who do not drink, and they do not eat. They breathe. It is said that the energy of the breath, and their Pranayama, is enough to sustain them. I met many fasting Sadhus named Urdhwavahurs, their skin paper-thin, their ribs poking out, but they were strong despite it all, with light in their eyes. Meditation can be so addictive that it is possible to see how you might want to stay in it forever, a bliss state. But I did not need to sit forever in this lifetime. I needed only to learn to sit.

Once I could be still, I began to listen. The plethora of songs in my head that had always been there quietened, and as my mind emptied, I heard everything as if for the first time. I heard an unfamiliar bird and looked up; it was a Kingfisher, with startlingly blue wings. I heard the rustling of the leaves in the wind, and the tiny trickle of the stream below. I could not pinpoint the exact moment that it happened, but somewhere in those mountains, I found God.

By God, I mean that I found a connection. I had never felt true harmony before; my life was always a little too fast, a bit off-kilter, and I had previously thought it was because I was too aware, too switched on to everything around me, and that simplicity and stillness was overrated. I was wrong. Harmony, for me, was to be found in finding peace.

I began to find new ways to find this feeling, this bliss state. I would light an incense stick and watch it until it burnt away, shaking off the ingrained feeling of impatience, of wasted time. I would draw patterns in the dirt and sand around me with my fingers and realise they were mandalas, that I was making a protective circle around myself from others, to mark out a spot where I could go to be undisturbed, to be still, and alone to think. I found peace on the motorbike, where my heart and the bikes engine were the same thing, transmuted into one energy, automatic and powerful. I found it in doing simple tasks with my eyes closed to attune my senses, chewing slowly, walking slowly, breathing slowly, moving slowly.

I noticed things more, little details like spider webs in morning dew, the softness of my skin, the taste of my morning coffee when I no longer rushed to finish it. I began to give thanks for my food, holding the plate in both hands before I took a bite. It wasn't that my God had a face or a name, it wasn't really faith, more of an overwhelming feeling that had been born in those fires of Varanasi and had steadily grown within me throughout my journey. It felt like a dissolution of fear.

Blackness was all that I had always envisaged after death, and so I realised that I had lived my life at a rocket-fast pace, desperate not to miss a minute. I always had a healthy level of respect for people who turned to prayer, but I never truly understood it, nor did I long for it. The problem was simply that I did not end or start the day with any sense of gratitude at all, not whether I was spiritual or not.

It did not matter that I was not thanking a person. To be

able to watch a sunset and think about all the things you have loved about that day is powerful, just as it is to wake up early to watch the sun rise, to reach a mountain temple and ponder who it was that lit the incense at the peak every day. Life took on more meaning when I was grateful for it.

Everything became more beautiful; even the rubbish piles that lined the railways coming into Delhi flooded me with feeling; the contrasting nature of being alive, with all the hardship and struggle, joy and beauty starting to merge into a single thread of consciousness, and it gave me purpose. I wasn't taking any drugs, I was not under the influence of a guru, or some cult. I was merely beginning to understand that I was such a tiny part of something so huge, and that there might be a reason for that. To have existed at all now filled me full of hope, and hope is one of the most comforting and powerful feelings of all.

KEDARNATH

I sit with a blanket on my lap and listen to the sounds of the temple.
Aarti rings out across every mountain top.
This chai wallah is steamy; a pot, constantly stirred, sits in the
middle over an open flame. The tea is never ending, topped up by
an old man who is singing mantras, and smiling, with two front
teeth missing. The people come and go, but I have been here for
hours since I first walked out in layers against the cold.

Upon hearing the temple's call, I tumble out of bed and sit on the
cold temple floor, pandits blessing my head with rose and jasmine. I
sit awhile with a Naga Sadhu naked but for a loin cloth, his body
smeared with ash. His touch is not cold. From time to time I see
him breathing; the pranayama keeping him warm, but he is
steadfast in his resolve to stay, though snowflakes threaten the air
with minus temperatures. He never takes his eyes from the temple,
only to bless those who have sat with him in his silence.

Kedarnath had been worth the climb and the excitement. Matt and I had wanted to do a pilgrimage for some time upon hearing that at the top of each trek stood some of the most auspicious temples. There were all kinds of spiritual pilgrimages that left from Rishikesh, but as this was just after the Indian lockdown, those were no longer operating, and the adventure was in finding them for ourselves. We started from a guesthouse at the bottom, with no warm water and the kind of Indian blankets one can only sympathise with if you've been to India. These were thick without being warm, synthetic, resembling floor carpet in an old hotel that has not been hoovered in a while, smelling faintly or sometimes strongly of armpits.

We set off at four o'clock in the morning, barely able to dress in the cold room, chiding ourselves for having packed far too much weight for the 11,000 feet climb. We got our passes at the bottom, which was a difficult thing to do in the wake of the first wave of Covid, as they were preventing foreigners from climbing and were only accepting Aadhar cards, the Indian identification. We called every Indian we knew and in minutes, we had everyone's biometric details from far and wide. Giggling at the relaxed attitude of Indians, we grinned and pushed our new Indian numbers through the tiny slot in the counter in the bustling queue, where our fingers swam in a sea of brown, handing over crumpled notes to the teller, and we were thankfully granted passage.

About three hours in, I realise I am the only woman walking this trek. The absence of women without the assistance of mules, clanging bells, and boys with sticks, is remarkable. Growing up in rural Britain, I looked around for my ladies in mountain boots and beanie hats. I saw only one.

"May I help you?" I asked as I went over to adjust her straps. Many teenagers have a habit of wearing their bags down incredibly low on their backs, and the sight of her huge heavy load being so unevenly distributed was irking me; she looked so tired. I shifted and pulled the straps to pull the load to her tiny frame.

"Much better," she said, smiling at me.

She was carrying the heaviest backpack of anyone I had seen so far. She was dressed in a pair of trainers, a thin jacket, and jeans, and did not, unlike every other traveller, carry a seventy-rupee cane, blessed with painted symbols, purchased obediently at the entrance. Her name was Priyanka.

"I left in a hurry, you see," she explained.

"Oh, me too," I sympathised, "...to catch the sunrise."

"No," she looked guiltily at me, "...not that. I left before my parents woke up."

Priyanka was about twenty, and, as it turned out, had left Mumbai during a global pandemic. She had defied her parents, travelled by train and bus over several states, and found her way here alone, to attempt a trek I was only a little curious about. She had dreamed about this her entire life, she told me, whilst I had come here on a bit of a whim. The gravity of my privilege hit me like a weight I was not wise enough to carry.

"It's not okay for me to be here," she said, "But I knew I had to come. I was called to."

I was glad to have such a powerful young woman with me. Trainers or not, she meant business. As my mind flew to my extra layers in my bag and I wondered what to offer her to keep warm, we met more young people along the way, excited to meet two women and just as dumbfounded to see us walking.

"You know you can take a mule?" they quizzed.

"Where's the fun in that?" we replied, winking at each other. As always, the feminist in me was bathing in the prospect of being an example to Indian men, changing the gender stereotypes they had been used to for so long, and stirring the pot a bit. Priyanka and I were subjected to questioning all the way along the mountain paths, being told to rest and being offered countless ponies to take our bags while the men we were with simply laughed at the failed attempts.

They had many questions for me about riding a motorbike as a woman, as they told Priyanka and I that we were doing something unique, inspiring, for women everywhere. I had not considered this. Priyanka's solo mission and my hazardous route were impressive feats in India, and probably many parts of the world. My upbringing in the UK and my free-spirited mother had never given me any indication me that I could not do whatever I wanted to. Priyanka and our group of men had shown me that for many Indian woman, this was a huge privilege. I vowed to treat it as such.

My friend Matteo was determined to make the most of this auspicious climb. He had fashioned a staff out of wood he had found, carved symbols into it, and attached an amethyst crystal to the top, which shone in the sunlight. The Indian boys found him fascinating. They looked to him as a leader, some sort of colourfully dressed white wizard, and asked him so many questions about Hindu mythology and spirituality so that five minutes in, I was grinning as I listened to them debating the famous stories, with a white man schooling the Indian boys about their Hindu philosophy.

We celebrated reaching about halfway. We ate some soggy Maggi noodles under a holey tarpaulin, masquerading as a dhaba, eating house, as the strong Himalayan rain lashed down, threatening to spoil our fun. Downing our tenth chai, we pressed on, bracing ourselves against the driving rain, and I looked sorrowfully at the tiny mules with their massive loads and their slipping hooves on the difficult paths. We added layers as we went, and reached glacier heights, where the temperature was starting to turn cold.

"It's snowing at the top," Indian tourists said on their way down, in denim jackets, expensive white trainers and thin t-shirts, their teeth chattering. They had flown up by helicopter, which was an option for those with a few more rupees in their pockets but they were totally unprepared for the cold descent. Others were barefoot, and sang devotional songs to keep spirits high, or told stories from scriptures, and talked of the wonders of the temple. My calves were about to give up entirely and some of us were quite breathless. It all went away in an instant when we glimpsed our first sight of Kedarnath temple at sunset.

The colours were as if I had put on special glasses. The greys accentuated the blue in the sky and the bright orange of the Shiva devotees dotted around the 8th-century temple, all backed by a blanket of white-dusted mountaintops and dark brown earth. It was hauntingly beautiful. A mantra was playing, which would be the only song that would play for the entirety of my time there, as I sat in tiny chai wallas and drank in the beauty of it. This temple did not look like one that had survived floods and glaciers, but she had spent almost four hundred years under the snow in a mini, or Chota ice age between the 13th and 17th centuries.

In India, many holy places are areas where a certain God or Goddess resided, reappeared as another form, or discarded parts of them, and these places are often in the Himalayas, at the highest points of India. The devotion of those who reach these places is absolute – often barefoot despite the freezing and broken ground, wearing only devotional lungis of the appropriate orange colour, singing mantras as they go.

It was incredibly humbling to watch people carry their

family members on their backs as an act of love. With only backpack straps and one which affixes to the forehead, often grandparents are carried, or those who are not able. The auspicious journey to Kedarnath means more to Hindu devotees of Shiva than I will ever be able to comprehend, some choosing it as their last dying wish to visit it.

I sat in awe as the Aarti bells called us to the temple and sat in the huddle of people as the Damru drum in the Pandit's hands rocked back and forth, representing the sound and energy of the universe. I gave thanks for my young body, that it had allowed me on this incredible journey, to see sights that most Indians could only dream of. Kedarnath was a life goal of many.

We cooked under the stars, in a little hut, wrapped in blankets against the whipping wind, and waiting for the pressure cooker to finish its whistles and puffs. The thali was one of the best I have ever tasted, and not just because of the lack of edible food on the ascent.

The owners of the guesthouse invited us to join their chanting, and we sat for what seemed like hours, with multiple voices ringing out into the night, the smell of sandalwood incense smoking in the freezing air. We did not undress, because the room was so cold that we could see our breath. We layered six of those famous armpit-scented blankets on top of us and slept the sleep of those at a high altitude, wakeful and full of dreams.

The next morning, as I walked alone across the temple grounds, I was hit immediately with the gravity of what I had done; just like Priyanka, Kedarnth had asked me to come, for what reason I did not know. I had not been aware that places such as these existed, so close to the sky, and for me, it was a vital shift in my understanding; it was the farthest I had ever been from the flat fields and grey streets of my homeland, and I could not believe that my world had revolved around grey concrete jungles for so long.

Shivering in the mountain air, I went off in search of a tandoor, a small fire. I stayed there all morning with elated people; they had not seen a foreigner for a year or more. We did not speak English; there was no need, each soul comfortable in the relative lack of communication, warming our hands over the same flames, blanketed and content and from all walks of life, together in a tiny hut at the top of the world.

The next day, we set off back down the trail, calves burning. There were hot springs at the bottom, and as we gratefully soaked our aching feet, we glimpsed the trail behind us, and realised the enormity of the trek that we had made. We got back to the bikes to find that all our bungee cords had been 'borrowed'. I told myself someone else had needed them more, as I tied my bag on with a strap made for one of the ponies. As I kicked my Avenger into gear, my legs were seizing up.

SUN AND MOON

One day later, we arrived at the base camp for Tungnath, one of the highest Shiva temples in India, at 12,073 feet, which was rumoured to be even more beautiful than Kedarnath. We had driven through towering pine forests, enjoying the hairpin bends and switchbacks which made our route akin to that of a racetrack. Most of the road was joyfully smooth, allowing for plenty of practice to hone our new skills and allowing us to push the speed, making ninety miles per hour on the even surfaces. We hauled our bags from our bikes once more, and limped past open fires and gloved villagers preparing food for the pilgrims at the bottom.

As we slept in another corrugated iron hut, condensation ran down the wall as Matt and I begrudgingly paid an extortionate 1000 rupees for the tin can accommodation. There was no hot water, so we strip-washed with a bucket in the freezing cold of the bathroom, and piled blankets on top of us once more in preparation for sleep. This time, they smelt unmistakably of cabbage. I awoke to realise that I could not stand up and was forced to shuffle hunch-backed, as my calves and hamstrings had seized up entirely, and would not straighten. Kedarnath had been more intense than I had realised. I had to admit defeat.

We changed our plan and jumped on the bikes again, driving to Badrinath at an altitude of 10,800 feet, another of the marked temples on the pilgrimage. To reach it, we had to pass over a dangerous mountain road, rife with the dreaded Maruti Suzuki's, but Matt and I had learnt how to handle our bikes by this point after all the practice, and were confident on the steep inclines, the broken surfaces, and the squeezing past of large vehicles which pushed us close to the edges. It was brightly coloured, with Tibetan wooden houses painted in kind, and the Alaknanda River that rushed through it, an astonishing, gleaming streak that sparkled in the sunlight. The village of Mana, above it, was one of the last villages in India before the borders of China and Tibet. We explored it for an afternoon, and saw the Tibetan people bundled up in wool, knitting in open doorways, who smiled at us with their eyes.

I had just begun to trust my bike when my back brake broke. The front brake was sensitive, and we were on gravel, rendering it quite useless in an emergency unless I wanted to career over the handlebars. I did not know at that time how to adjust it or fix the back brake. There were no mechanics for miles, and so I set off down a very steep decline, braking gently and often, in first gear. It didn't make much of a difference, as the path was so steep and slippery with gravel that the speed of the bike soon crept up to fifty miles an hour on the slopes and slid dangerously whenever the brake was hesitantly applied.

There was nothing for it but to risk it, as I could not leave the bike in the open, and it was getting dark. Luckily, anyone who had any sense or knew the road had packed up an hour before, and the one path home was now deserted, leaving me to take a little more risk and zoom down the paths in the dark. I chided myself for not having worn leg protection, but my jacket had protected me thus far. After the accident less than a week before and having little choice but to ride a broken bike, I was beginning to realise that I had been a little naïve in setting off with such a lack of motorcycle knowledge.

We hit concrete again, and I stopped for a moment to catch my breath and steady my nerves. The rest of the route in the darkness was an incredible thrill, but comfortably so, turning bend after hairpin bend, on deliciously soft tarmac, leaning into the curves. It was the road of dreams for any biker. We pulled into a dhaba at the side of the road to refuel and they offered us a bed for the night which we collapsed into gratefully.

We started the trek to Tungnath the very next day, and set off at sunrise, the sky already tangerine and lilac colours with wisps of clouds. It was perfect weather for climbing, and as we ascended into the forest, it was deathly quiet. The trek to Kedarnath had been vibrating with excitable energy, but we walked in silence for four straight hours.

At the top, I visited the Shiva temple. A man kindly took my hand and placed it on the ears of Nandi, Shiva's bull, the protector deity of Shiva situated in front of the temple. He educated me on the practice of Shrungadarshan, explaining that the stone carving, Shiva lingam, which is present at all Shiva temples, was too powerful to be viewed alone, and that Nandi's ears and my fingers created a divine window through which the energy of Shiva and Shakti could be absorbed. He explained that nature is always in duality, with Shiva and Shakti representing the masculine and feminine in life. The man then told me to whisper my wishes in the ears of Nandi, and that they would come true. I whispered many.

There is a story in Indian mythology about Lord Shiva, one of the creators of the world. It tells how the local men jealously cursed his lingam. When it dropped to the floor, it began to destroy the earth. He took it back upon a promise that the people would worship his lingam. Honouring a penis had not been on my list of Indian experiences, but I decided to have a go.

We climbed higher, to a second temple. The temple was barely big enough to crawl into, and people had left offerings in a small window. It was eerily silent on the peak, except for a bell which we rang. Temple bells are said to steady you, to calm the mind and soul before meditation, or prayer. It also brings you back into awareness, for those who could meditate forever.

As I sat with my friend Matt and meditated, the urge to sing came. We sang soft mantras, and tears ran down my face in gratitude, as I watched the moon and sun rise in opposite sides of the sky. Charcoal mountains were on all sides, a perfect panoramic view. They were dusted with icing sugar sprinkles. We were sitting on cotton clouds as the view disappeared underneath our feet. The sky burnt the deepest red that I have ever seen, and people began to leave. I could not.

I believe that the energy of some places is nearly impossible to leave, and that the energy of everyone who has passed through stays, in some way. I feel that if it is a place that has seen a lot of pure intention, the peace is palpable. I could have stayed at Tungnath for days, to sit in the tranquillity. Matt dragged me away as night fell, and we walked down the mountain in the pitch black, with no lights. We heard wolves, and looked at each other, not that I could see his eyes. We quickened our pace, and with relief, saw the entry gate. We rang the bell as we completed our trek, and collapsed back into our cabbage-scented beds.

As we marked out the map for the return journey, I knew that it was time to leave the mountains. I was ready to see more of India. I had seen mountains crumble in front of my wheels, had told my secrets to the Gods, I had meditated on the tops of snowy peaks, and most of all, I had experienced the thrill of my first motorcycle trip, and in the Himalayas no less.

I mounted my rented Avenger for the last time and set off for the last stretch home, enjoying the hours of broken roads. I pulled into sleepy Rishikesh after dark the next evening and into the arms of John, realising I was wearing broken prescription glasses, torn jeans, and so covered in dust that my eyebrows were almost welded together.

I did not know what was next for me as I packed my bags, said goodbye to my favourite cow, and got ready to board a train to Goa, but I remember thinking that I would not find adventures such as these again. How wrong I was; India was not finished with me yet.

GOA CALLING

As the train doors clatter, the chill tugs at my thin blanket as we
rush through the cold night. I lie on a three-class bed of iron, barred
windows, a flickering lightbulb. We hide the snacks; the mice would
make light work of peanuts and potato crisps, our thirsty mouths
too salted to finish them. My lover and I, too restless to sleep, smoke
a joint out of the swinging carriage door, one on the lookout, and
steal kisses in between drags, one foot on the parapet, the other
holding balance. As the train slows, we jump and marvel at the gap.
The moon has rings around her, rouge against pearlescent, in a
smoked and charred sky.

The cold air stings our cheeks as engines once again roar to life and
we run to grasp at handles to pull ourselves up the steps, the ground
rushing beneath, laughing deep in our bellies. The monotonous,
familiar chanting of "chai, chai," floats in and out of earshot as
gentle snores and the knocking of straps and chains tease the
sleeping mind into awareness.
I look up at sleeping bodies above me, pure joy washing over my
whole body like the warm Goan sea which beckons us, as we
squeeze tighter into tiny curls to keep the heat, beanies on. It is two

o'clock in the morning, with the remnants of caffeine still whispering in my bones, the jostling of the rails and the clatter of the tracks as I lie with my head on my pack, and look at my lover, bleary-eyed and sleepy across the aisle turning in for the night.

Sharp stops and slamming of brakes shake and sneak open my windowpane as I begin to dream, and the train quietens her pace. I hear the patter of more running feet, as many more hands fasten and snatch at train door handles, to catch it in time.

ROMANCE

"You're lovely," I said.
"I love you too," he replied, as we sat to watch the sunset with now-
widening eyes, and I could not stifle my smile and screamed a little;
outwardly, not inside.
If rainbow-coloured clouds surrounding that gelatinous red sun
can hide her beaming glow, then I cannot, when I know that he
loves me. He loves me.
If all the stars fell out of the sky, I would still be shining brightly
for all the galaxies to see. If we are two such stars, then let us fall
together, shooting across the black, as one burning, bright arc.

ARAMBOL

Warm, balmy days leaked into weeks and then months. The air at night did not move, though we were so close to the beach that we could hear the waves crashing on the shore. The ground felt like a heavy dark carpet underneath my feet, and I for one was reluctant to dive in.

Arambol, in Goa, reeked of sex, hard liquor, sun cream and string bikinis, a far cry from the meditative states of the North of India. I was alone in this; my little community flourished in the sea, salt and sun and quickly settled into their routine of lazy days and heat-soaked nights. I was not ready for a return to the western world just yet, and Arambol felt a little too like a bedazzled festival.

I did not know how to be still, then. I had only just learnt how to sit with myself, and my world on arrival into Arambol had been shaken up like a two for one cocktail offer in one of the beachside bamboo shacks. The hangovers from the night before were breaking the healthy patterns so easily acquired in the mountains, the early rises and daily walks made harder by the arrival of the merciless sun, already reaching its peak at eight am.

We had everything at our disposal and wanted for nothing. We even had a therapist with us. Liesl, an earthy and motherly South African with a wicked sense of humour, supported the community as we experienced many more months away from our homes all over the world. I went to her often for guidance, and the reason I liked her was because she was so matter of fact and knew if you were making excuses.

Liesl would hold community circles like those that I experienced with Gagori, and we would investigate together what it meant to be alive, and to ponder the bigger picture. She had a knack of choosing a topic every week that resonated with all of us, so much so that I often found my mouth wide open. It was what many of us needed; a completely safe space to ask all the questions we had ever desired. Liesl did not offer all the answers, only more questions.

I thought back to therapy in the UK, how private a topic it was, how we often talked of it in hushed voices behind the backs of our hands and paid for it privately so that we did not have to tell the family doctor. At the end of six to twelve sessions, prescribed only after a meltdown of some kind, you are often on your own to navigate life. Liesl's sessions were offered by donation; she said that communities start by spreading seeds, and suggested that we scatter our own one day, to give back what we had received.

With no new tourists coming into the country as restrictions held, accommodation was offered at ridiculous prices. All the rooms that we had stayed in so far had been heavily discounted, and we were paying less than one hundred English pounds a month, or 9,000 rupees, for which we were very grateful – most of the community had been struggling after nine months of lockdown with no work and no certainty of returning to their own countries.

The situation in Arambol was like Rishikesh, in that there had been no actual reported cases of Covid. People would text each other to send an alert when the police came into town to check masks, but other than that, none of the locals wore anything on their faces which was an incredible luxury.

There were days when I struggled. I would lie on my bed under the mosquito net and stare at the ceiling, hoping for the lockdown to calm down in the big cities so that I could return to the cold where I felt I belonged. I started to pick up old habits that I thought I had lost, biting my nails and fingers until they bled, anxiety pulling at my core and begging to be settled; I wanted to move again, I wanted the mountains, I wanted the North. I was not connected to anything here; I longed for the culture that Northern India had shown me, looked for meaning deeper than I could get from my daily yoga class and prayed for the backs of my knees to stop sweating.

I finally shook myself out of the Kapha, calm state of Goa and bought a massage table and began to take up work again, with plenty of clients. My purpose came back, as I remembered how it felt to use my hands and everything that Gagori had taught me, and what it felt like to be in meditative states of peace after a session.

I returned to myself once more, filled with purpose. I was inundated with business, Arambol's culture of relaxation aiding me immensely. As word spread, I became known for my work and wherever I moved to, people would ask for appointments; Gagori's teachings and her unique massage speaking for itself. The local coconut oil was abundant and smelt incredible, and every penny of the massage went back into my pocket or that of the fruit seller down the road, who kept me in bananas. It was a fortuitous and easy existence.

There was one thing above all else that kept me in Goa. John. We lived in separate houses but across the road, allowing for late-night tapping at windows and balconies, and morning lie-ins, stark-naked under the canopy of the palm trees. I wrote erotica about our lovemaking, and he served me coffee while I wrote.

It was a beautiful and addictive existence and would have been all-consuming if it were not for the elephant in the room; John was going back to his homeland, for some time. Thus, a travelling relationship was born, both desperate not to attach, and committing instead only to loving each other, for as little or as long a time as we both had.

I got attached, of course. I had managed to find a man who was checking every box on a little list I had written in Rishikesh when I was ready to love again. My heart had already decided that he was mine. Every few weeks we would try to shake each other off, and fall back together again, waking up in puddles of passion, roaring laughter, scintillating debates and deep, beautiful connection. It was no good; infatuated from the start, we could only enjoy each other. He would become my very best friend, my biggest fan, and in the end, would push me to the edges of what I thought was possible in my capacity to love.

It is a strange thing, to love when there is an expiration date, and to love anyway. In a way, I think it encourages you to live for the moment, acutely aware that at any moment it may be snatched away.

Every man I had met in India had broken the mould of what I had been used to. A far cry from my dating history of men who seemed to mainly be entangled in the apron strings of their mothers, John fascinated me. He was a feminist, an environmentalist, and fiercely independent. More than anything, John would open me to something that India had been trying to teach me all year: how to let my wild side in.

JELLYFISH

I don't remember who suggested that we took acid, but it was probably not me. We found ourselves one night on a secret beach about to do that very thing. We erected a shelter, prepared food, made a gigantic fire, removed our clothes, and took one final breath together, holding hands and setting intentions before popping the little tabs under our tongues.

I watched the crabs scuttling in the sand, and when I started drawing lines in between them to turn them into DNA, I knew I was tripping. This was my first ever trip; the 'good girl' archetype falling all around me like the ash from the burning ghats. Initial nausea surprised me as the world spun a bit, and suddenly we were all spinning together, round and round in ecstatic laughter, on a never-ending search for cigarettes to take the edge off, which never appeared, and water which had been responsibly sourced but never drunk. We raced into the sea to feel the waves on our naked skin, and as we stood admiring the fading sunset into blacking skies, I was hit with a lashing of pain.

It had grabbed me like a cat-o-nine-tails, slashing around

the back of my leg and holding me in its grip. John was hit, too, and as we physically attacked our friends behind us to get them out of the water, they, incredibly, escaped with no injuries at all. We inspected at John who had a welt on his leg, and then they looked at me. The jellyfish had burnt a handprint into my skin. Red raw and blistering, it was visible by the light of the fire.

I howled with pain as they grimaced at it, as I laughed insanely to anyone who would listen that this was a symbol of control, of me holding on too tightly to my life, that this handprint was my lesson, I had to let go. The fire helped a little, the heat taking away the sting. My friend in his altered state turned into a Shaman, sucking out the poison with his hands and mumbling incantations. I was in excruciating pain until they urinated on me. There is no evidence to suggest that peeing on anyone helps at all, but in our altered states, it was all that we could think of, and we treated it like drops from heaven.

My friend Anaelle was first; pee sprung from between her legs like an elixir of life, we cupped our hands underneath her and roared with laughter between the streams, insisting that the other take the pain-relieving fluid, slapping it onto our legs like the medicine it apparently was. Daniel had found the five-litre canteen and was slopping it down his front like a man possessed, to hydrate, and thus provide for us.

He shouted in exasperation, as we hovered beneath him, stage fright preventing flow.

"Please pee on her!" John begged, flailing around in pain himself, as Daniel peed directly onto my leg, not only splashing me but into the face of Anaelle, laid by the fire.

None of us could breathe for laughing, the absurdity of the night and our own versions of reality changing with every passing minute. Daniel turned into a clown in front of my eyes, while Anaelle became a princess. The next minute, she was pregnant with a belly of sand. Daniel roared like a lion and beat his chest, snarling and emitting terrifying growls to a ceiling of black above him.

The handprint grew ever brighter in the light of the flames, which is possibly what was helping with the pain, and not the urine. I walked directly over the ashes at one point and did not feel a thing, the sting always occupying my mind. It went to my heart then and became a chest full of biting insects, the most intense pain that I had ever experienced. I took myself away to deal with it, gathering firewood, determined to ride it out alone, my hands in fists, jaw clenched.

John had become the caretaker, and had been building the enormous fire, cooking vegetables for us in tinfoil, in the hot ashes. I was ravenous but could not eat, and instead watched the others as they devoured the feast, smiles of ecstasy on their faces. As Anaelle and I cuddled each other like sisters for the come down, we grew sleepy and retired to the fireside, underneath billions of stars in an opaque sky.

When sunrise came, with the embers of our mighty fire still warm, I sat up and looked around me at my lover sleeping next to me and at the peace of the morning. The beach was deserted. I inspected my leg. The pain, strangely, after being so intense, now only stung a little. The mark was still there; it was a handprint after all; five fingers, or purple tendrils, wrapped around me in perfect form. I wondered why only two of us had been affected, but something hit me even harder. In this situation, we had all shown our most powerful traits. My capacity to hold great pain. John as a masculine protector of us all. My married friends had become a united team working together. My first trip on acid was a huge test of the mind and body and I had understood the lesson. It was time to let go of expectations, and of what I could not control in my life, instead of holding on so tightly to everything. Like the snake in my visions in Rishikesh, perhaps it was time to shed my skin.

ONE YEAR IN INDIA

The apartment was filled with dust and had stood empty for some time. A Goan family whose livelihood had been ravaged by monsoon storms did not understand why I wanted to live here at all, in the great shadow of the new and spacious apartment next door which was offered for the same cheap-as-chips price. The beams were littered with enormous spider webs, the shower both only dripped and electrocuted my head, and there was a bird of a noisy kind singing songs of protest on the tree outside. I was in love with the place from the moment I set eyes on the attic.

It was thrilling to me, the idea of living somewhere so cheaply which truly resembled a home. Up until now, the guesthouses had been wonderful but were temporary spaces. It had not dawned on me until this point that people lived like this permanently. Some people moved to India, and this was how they survived. It was easy, I could see that now. My mind was blown, coming from a country where half my pay packet each month was spent on rent and bus fare and bills, split between deciding whether to blow it all on Friday night drinks to distract from the stress or buying a new pair of work shoes for the job I disliked. It was all beginning to make sense to me now. I could live differently.

I had inadvertently managed to plonk myself into the heart of Russian territory, which in any other time except Covid would have been party city. It was the former home of constant trance blasting through the sea air from tinny speakers, discarded vodka bottles in the sun-parched grass and sunrise toasts to congratulate each other on their various states of drunkenness, but now there were only five Russians in the whole of the area and, thankfully, only one mini speaker. The balconies backed on to each other, whole lives lived inside tiny apartments, a whole world of cultures in one street. There was a guitar-playing elderly Indian who sat on his porch playing Bon Jovi and Johnny Cash, a samosa seller on a bicycle with a horn loud enough to cross oceans, a French nymphomaniac who liked to peek at John and I half-dressed on our balcony, and a huge pack of street dogs, the like of which I have never heard again, their incessant barking the worst that I have endured in all of India, thieves of my sleep for four long months.

Mango Season was tailing off in the South, but we had arrived just in time, with many colours of mangoes piled at the sides of every road. I sat with friends gorging ourselves from the fruit carts. They were ripe and bursting, their flesh orange, and their outsides a gorgeous mix of yellow and tropical green and made your mouth water just to look at them. Unlike a watermelon, which requires a bit of skill to pick, every mango from every cart was fantastic, but you had to be careful not to pick the green sour ones accidentally, which are used to make pickle.

I ate my mangoes still warm from the sun, usually in the bathroom over the sink or in the shower, to ward off the exceptionally fast invasion of ants, and threw the peels to the pigs below. The advantage of living in that apartment was that there was absolutely no need for a bin; my diet was fresh fruit and vegetables, and all waste was chucked over the balcony. It was very eco-friendly.

My neighbour was a girl from Canada whom I had affectionately named just the same, who loved to be naked on her balcony and play loud early-morning hip-hop. Just being around her had a very grounding effect on a person. Canada was a nude model for several Indians who probably could not believe their luck at being able to photograph such a beauty in all her nakedness. She had an infectious laugh and a fantastic sense of humour and had been a neighbour in most of my chosen accommodations, from jungle dwellings to dark hotel rooms with mouldy wardrobes.

As we made ourselves more at home, Canada and I cooked on real gas burners and enjoyed the luxury of a fridge for the first time. We made Canadian pancakes on Christmas morning and donned Christmas hats found in the back of a tiny shop. The local Christian church put fairy lights on a tree, but Goa was otherwise undecorated, the only indication of celebrations being the tradition of hunting the local pigs, which they shot and roasted in full sight, on the side of the road, while I covered my ears and eyes.

John made me a stocking and I bought him a cricket bat. We celebrated with a group of friends, with everyone bringing food from their country, and copious amounts of alcohol. My lockdown family and their warmth eased the pain of leaving my own family at home. I breathed out the guilt at not waking up on Christmas morning at my mother's house, as I had done for thirty-two years without fail, and realised that it had become another attachment that I was unable to let go of. I had no choice this year but to be in India. Gagori had told me to let go of that which I could not control.

As we introduced more food into the long-discarded attic

apartments, Canada noticed an enormous bite mark had been taken out of a watermelon. Large paw-prints also appeared on my walls next door and then disappeared to the roof, and thus the speculation and amusement began as to whether our non-rent-paying neighbour was a lizard, cat, or rat. On one such night, we came home to see it scuttling through her window, the long tail slinking through the gap, and the truth was revealed; the sound of a startled Canadian would then come through the whisper-thin walls for weeks, accompanied by an audible gasp at the size of the bites it had taken out of various pantry items or disturbing it mid feast in the middle of the night. It would be in my room that the big old rat finally took its last gigantic footsteps, perhaps having drunk itself to death from fruit, or, like most animals in India, eating plastic.

We scooped it into a pizza box with a broom and sang it a mantra, and it was then dutifully fed to the pigs by the landlord. We realised afterwards that he had poisoned it, and now possibly the pig who had it for dinner, who they would then eat, but as with everything in India, there was no point questioning anything; people fed cows last night's thali and the cure for worries was a chillum.

Those Goan nights in the sweltering heat with a beer in my hand, lying with Canada listening out for creatures in the eves, was the only time in my life where I felt completely devoid of responsibility, completely at ease with not knowing what was coming next. I realised with a jolt that I had never done this. I had never been out of a nine to five job for over sixteen years, I had never had the opportunity to be still, and it was incredibly liberating. I was making enough to survive on and no more, but I now knew that I could also live with much less. I remembered working sixty hours a week and being paid for half of that, and almost crumbling in the process. It reminded me of something that Gagori had once said.

"Every day we walk to our grave so quickly."

I was choosing to slow down now, determined to enjoy my life. The fast pace of England was a distant memory. I was shedding my old patterns and conditioning like the mangoes fell, abundantly. Living on very little, the simplicity and no-frills attitudes of Indian life suited me. The fast-fashion, must-have-it, ego-driven consumerism of the world had always bothered me; India so far had fitted me like one of my worn old shoes, comfortable and already moulded to my shape.

After three months, many massage clients, and after celebrating one year of being 'stranded' in India, I had saved enough money to leave Goa. I bade farewell to my home, the sparkling sea, and to a brand-new rat in the eves. My leaving prompted John to follow, and we mounted a motorbike and dived back into the India that I knew best, the raw and lovable messiness.

HAMPII

Two rocks, as if they had hands, held the reddening sun in their thumb and forefinger and helped it sink between two great boulders.

The silence came, as it always does at first when the sun goes down. A kind of hush, like the birds know, and the trees, and all have held their breath. When they let it out, it is a cacophony of agreement: this, as every night, is the most magnificent they have ever seen. It is as if the whole blanket of the jungle has applied a silencer, and muffled cries ring across the branches, in quiet respect of the night to come. We breathe out too, as the rock, warmed by the sun, begins to lose its heat, and warnings of leopards play on wandering minds. Backs to the rock face, atop the highest of perches; we are the perfect kill, for something wanting to hunt.

Footsteps pound the paths below, but we are alone here, atop this heavy boulder and enviable stillness, where interestingly flavoured birds soar and dip their wingtips to touch our foreheads. In the distance, agile, sumptuous, perfume-scented notes of sitar and harmonium ring across the sky, the Mughal ruins fall into shadow, and the clattering of tin signals Puja at the temple.

The rock does not get colder, despite the lateness of the hour. As darkness beckons, the trills and chirps from the creatures among the cacti fade.

I feel as if I will never see a sight like this again, and gratefulness washes over me like the mist that comes ever closer, settling in for the chilly morning where sunrise will awaken the jungle in amber light. As the tree-line fades to black, the air thickens somehow and clings around us, holds onto our very bones, as if we too are being tucked in for the night, to dream of Jurassic stone and the temple-dotted fields, of Hampii.

GIRL ON A BIKE

The feminist in me wanted to drive; the romantic in me wanted to be on the back of his motorbike forever, in flowing skirts and braided waist-length hair, bare legs and hennaed feet, arms around his waist as he expertly handles 'Pushkarini'.

She was a black 'Bullet', 350cc with most of her chrome still shining, his dream of owning a classic Royal Enfield motorbike come true. We named her on a road in the jungle, her name inspired by the beautiful temple baths of Hampii, with whisky sipped from a one-hundred-rupee bottle which we had splashed on her front to bless her.

Save for our rest days, the reality of being the girl on the back was not the epic romance I had imagined; hot helmets and no air, thick oversized jeans and boots protected us from the road, flannel shirts kept the raging sun from our backs, thick dust clung to eyebrows and transformed our faces, settling in every line, the journey harsh in the hot climate. We dipped our clothes in streams and under taps at the side of the road, to keep cool, and the salt from our sweat mixed with the sun and bleached our shirts, pale white sun cream splashed across necks. It was liberating, to such be a mess, but far from the glamour I had envisaged.

The villages that we passed in Karnataka, in the South-West of India, turned more rural, and we saw what most tourists could only dream of seeing; real India, where women in cotton saris washed their clothes in the road and villagers spread out fruits and vegetables on long grasses under the trees to dry. I saw them farming, metal, and wood ploughs turning the fields, pulled by enormous and loping water buffalo.

John gave me a turn to drive, and I marvelled at the feel of Pushkarini, her engine smooth but for her adorable way of cutting out over a big bump. I recalled the fast bends on that Avenger some months ago, the crash, the near misses, and most of all, the rush of freedom. I knew that it was time to try and find my own, because to be whisked away by a lover, no matter how romantic, is still without the total freedom of driving solo.

BULLET

Ullu was originally named 'Unicorn', perhaps chosen by the mechanic himself. She was a 2009 Royal Enfield Machismo 350 – a classic, but dated motorbike in military green, and who caused me no end of grief but whom I loved dearly, and what we experienced together became a monumental part of my journey in India. I named her Ullu, after the steed of Goddess Lakshmi, the Goddess of wealth and prosperity, a great white owl who was auspiciously chosen to send Lakshmi into battle against her foes.

I remember the first time I lay eyes on her outside a mechanics, with her seat torn and her chrome rusted, and I remember thinking to myself that this was one of the most beautiful things I had ever seen. The mechanic smiled a little too hard as he quoted me, and as I knocked ten thousand rupees off the original price, I knew it was still too much. Using the ten I knocked off for parts, he did a lazy job on her, leaving so many bits un-tuned and without the full check that I had asked for.

The bike was so rusted and raw from being left out in the Goan sun and humidity that it was a wonder she ran at all.

She was a 'Daddi' bike, an old lady of a machine. Eventually she ran out of steam after so long being ignored, giving me the opportunity which I never knew I needed which was to learn how a motorbike operated.

When I bought her, I had known nothing about motorcycles. Had I had the money, I would perhaps have gotten a newer model, but then I would have learnt nothing with no breakdowns, and with no risk attached. My lover laughed when I bought it and she rattled on the way home, and as we realised just how much rust was on her chrome, he told me stories of his dad's workshop at home in South Africa and their beloved Jeeps, where every trip would end in a breakdown. He assured me that this bike I had fallen for would require constant maintenance, but that nothing in the world would ever give me the feeling that this Enfield would. He was right on both counts.

I needed some riding gear. The little Honda Navi, a kind of hybrid bright-yellow toy-size bike I had been zipping around on for the last few months, had not required any padding of any kind, but riding through cities is notoriously more dangerous in India than the countryside, and we were going to pass through New Delhi, India's capital. I went to a mall for the first time in my entire India experience, which was both frightening and confusing to me after months away from modern life and looked for a few simple items; a pair of sturdy jeans that might help me to survive a potential fall, and some long sleeves, to beat the sun.

I think I must have tried five shops before becoming exasperated at the lack of jeans with any merit, instead being subjected to wafer-thin, body-hugging leggings. I could not find a pair of decent trousers anywhere, not even in the sports section, and everything was pink. A light bulb moment hit, and I charged up the stairs to the men's department, where I was presented with about fifteen types of jeans, all relatively thick. When I asked about jeans for biking, I was immediately pointed to a section with embroidered patches sewn on all the clothes. This was unbelievable; it was so easy to get what you needed as a biker here, but only as a man.

As I grabbed some jeans in my equivalent size, I passed a rail with t-shirts covered in motivational slogans, like,

'You're the boss,' and, 'Adventures Await'.

I thought back sadly to the neon outfits I had seen in the women's section, with slogans like, 'Beauty Queen,' and 'Princess.'

I was kidding myself if I believed there would be many women riders in India – it was clear now that not only was it not encouraged, but it was made actively difficult to become one. I took my purchases to the payment counter.

"For your husband?" smiled the salesperson, sweetly.

GOA TO DELHI

We rolled up to the station one dusky morning and cut the engines, aware that time was very short. India's second lockdown was shutting down everything behind us, and we were determined not to get caught up in its wake. Everything and everyone seemed as if it was in a hurry, but perhaps it was only that way for John and me as we snatched our bags from the motors and hauled them to the side of the parcel packing doorway.

We thrust our passports into the hands of men flitting about the place and looked for paper copies of our visas to give to the station master. The station master was dressed in a beige khaki uniform top and tracksuit pants and sat behind a plastic screen with a scratched window, with one of those voice holes that one would go nowhere near in the time of Covid 19. Instead of using this, however, he motioned for me to join him in his office on a little mismatched stool with a wonky fourth leg, and started asking me all kinds of questions, jotting them down in his enormous ledger book which looked hundreds of years old and was falling apart at the binding.

The questions were not relevant to my situation at all, but I realised that they were simply a status thing, the sort of situation I was now used to and would repeat again multiple times before the end of my journey in India. It was to appease, to pay my dues as a white foreigner coming through his train station, and I caught on to this quickly, firing answers back more readily than he could scribe into that brick of a book. It was the same old tired questions; name, country of origin, did I follow cricket or football, preceded by the names of multiple players of each sport in a sort of order until I, realising I was now in a never-ending trap of sporting surnames, nodded profusely at one of them and said, "Oh yes, good batter,"

It was a good guess, and we were both allowed through to the next round, which was to board the train.

Five copies of each document were made, and there was a mystery fee, as this was pronounced a special train. It was indeed, as it miraculously had room enough in the carriage for both our bikes, and had we decided to leave Goa in the following days, we would not have made it at all but for this extra carriage.

As John expertly took off our mirrors and the team ran the engines dry for the journey, we watched them wrap the bikes in reels of dusty cloth, writing on our names and passport numbers in fat marker pen, as the Indian post office did. We bade our beloved engines goodbye and hauled our heavy bags to the station entrance. The train master followed us to the platform, putting two hundred rupees into my hand and shaking it. I think he felt bad about the extra charge. This kind of act of kindness is one that I have seen so often in India now that it is easy to forget them all, but this was one that stayed with me.

At Delhi, some thirty hours of train ride later, we crossed miles of platforms with our luggage, neither of us having the sense to hire a porter. I think it's that sense of privilege that knocks you sideways sometimes, which forces most people with a good heart to refrain from partaking in any services which require any back-breaking work on the part of an Indian. The service was ridiculously cheap, to have your bags carried on the heads and shoulders of men working the sides of the railways, and it is often a complete moral dilemma as to whether to take them up on this and give them work or carry them yourself for fear of being labelled privileged, and to have that twisty gut feeling that you are taking advantage.

I recalled one of my first jaw-dropping moments in India, watching a wife carry her husband's colossal suitcase on top of her head, her arms holding two shopping bags as he texted on his phone. I remember being appalled and impressed. Indian women are some of the strongest and most resilient people I will ever meet, and they always carry the heaviest loads, whether in the mountains or the cities.

The women I had ridden past in the farmlands on the way to the station were so hunch-backed that they could not walk upright but were bent double, chest to the knees, hay bales on their backs. The sight of them would make me sad at first, but their strength was something I would always remember, in times of my own struggle. It was a beautiful mirror; back in the UK I had been carrying my own heavy load, but their load was evidently ten times the size of mine in many ways. I thought about how I had often felt like that as a white foreigner in India; and how India was often a reflection of everything I could not appreciate about my life, everything that I took for granted.

Two hours after disembarking from the train and standing in queues of people, attempting to communicate in broken Hindi, we were taken to the correct spot to retrieve the bikes, which was at the other end of the station once more. Wheeling them across the narrow pathways between the rails took skill in the midday heat which was beating down hard on us amid the polluted capital, but we finally got them to the road to meet up with our backpacks which we had left in a pile. After all the bits and pieces had been fixed on to precision, and possibly-watered-down fuel had been sourced, we were good to go.

We were not under any illusion in our haste; Delhi, too, was locking down. It was in the air, the urgency of the people, the hurried steps and dropped packages, the sold-out trains, the masks on every face. I reminded myself that we would not be here any longer than necessary, but it was certainly strange to be entering the capital city from which everyone was fleeing. Covid was in Delhi, all right. News of oxygen tank shortages were on the newspapers at the samosa stand, tales of funeral pyres unable to cope with the millions of dead had been passed from train bunk to train bunk.

Our idea was to get across Delhi and out of the district entirely before anyone could make us quarantine in all that madness. Darkness threatened, and as we switched on our lights in five-lane traffic, dodging and swerving at two-second intervals and with my hand in serious cramp from controlling the clutch so often, we finally made it to our hotel for the night on the outskirts of Delhi, and collapsed onto the stained mattress, barely-dripping showered and rough-towelled.

John snapped into action and spooned oats and peanut butter into my exhausted mouth as we realised neither of us had anticipated that a closing Delhi also meant closed dhabas. Our reality hit us then. I thought about how we were still at risk of being locked down in whichever city we were unfortunate enough to be passing by, and as tempting as it would be to lie in the following morning and sleep away the previous day and night's stiffness in the joints, it could be costly if we did not make it across the Haryana border.

Infused with only the will not to be captured, we put our heads down for a few hours sleep and rose again, tired but determined.

The plan was quite simple. We decided to stay off the main roads, for fear of being stopped by the police. Not only was my bike an eyesore with peeling paint, but as she was in military green, she caught the eye of everyone on the road. Topped with a female rider, she got plenty of unwarranted attention. I decided that covering my entire face was the only option, and wore layers to hide my shape, which helped a little; the first was useful in the Delhi sun, and the second was not. Dripping with sweat, we panicked for a moment as we came to a standstill and believed the road had been cordoned off entirely, but it was a large protest of farmers, and the route to Haryana was still open.

Our route would have been a simple one but for going through Haryana and Punjab, as we checked the list of cities under lockdown which was increasing one by one along our planned drive and thought it best not to try our luck riding through them. We took the back roads, feeling like outcasts.

In Haryana, we happened upon one of the worst storms I had ever had to ride through. The difference in heat between the two states caused blinding sandstorms there often. I marvelled at Ullu's strength, as she held her own in winds buffeting even John and Pushkarini from side to side.

I felt such gratitude for this bike; each other's quirks had yet to be discovered yet she still felt completely safe to me, this noble steed carrying me through conditions which my inexperienced hands did not know how to weather.

This did not last for long. I dumped Ullu on the side of the road as a long piece of electrical wire dropped into the road and caught both of my handlebars. To this day I cannot say where it came from or what it was attached to, but it was one of the most dangerous things you can imagine, though quite normal for India. John had ducked expertly, his years of experience on the road serving him well, and I saw him looking back as I fell, entangled, her rusty cap leaking petrol onto the side of the road as trucks blared their horns impatiently. I wondered how I would ever get her back up again, as I had not yet developed the strength in my arms to even attempt it. Luckily, Indians have seen everything, and the two nearest bystanders jumped into action, lifting her in an instant and giving me a clap on the back as I mounted her again, sending me on my way. Ullu started immediately, a beast of a machine, and she glided triumphantly down the pilled and pocketed roads of Punjab until we got to a police checkpoint near the base of the next state, Himachal Pradesh.

This was the first checkpoint that we had encountered, and so we did not want to stop for fear that they would hold us up or find out we were from Goa, for fear of being locked in Haryana. We drove at a steady speed, and John passed the gate. Out of nowhere, an official of some kind came flying down the hillside in casual clothing and threw himself at Ullu's handlebars, snatching at her mirrors to stop me. I was probably doing thirty-five miles an hour, having not yet reached anywhere near the entrance to the checkpoint, and was in third gear. I shook him off, but it also shook me up entirely. The officers saw the whole scene and did not interject or slow me down, but I then hit the throttle instinctively and flew through the checkpoint to freedom, leaving only dust, and screaming an Indian expletive into the wind.

News of others trying to leave Goa hit us in various forms. Cancelled trains and flights were sent to us by text, our community not having known our exact plans and sending us warnings. I thanked my lucky stars that we had had the gumption to take the earlier train, and we watched the news in our new hotel room to find that lockdown was rapidly spreading across Haryana, Delhi, and Punjab too. It was a race against time, but we were winning.

We finally crossed the border that night to Himachal Pradesh, and as we started to climb the hills towards cooler air and calmer villages, I found myself half in prayer as I felt cold wind in my hair at last. This northern girl from England was on her way back home to the North once more, and I felt it, imagining the tapestry of nature that would soon come, forest and streams and cold winds, gloved hands.

We slept that night in a hotel which reinforced our fears of the lockdown as they almost refused us, on the grounds that our visas, currently in process by the Indian FRRO, or Foreigner Regional Registration Officers, were almost expired. The government was deliberating what to do with all the foreigners who had been trapped for so long, and it was taking weeks to get a visa, which we had to apply for every month. No one was moving on those grounds, accepting their fate to stay wherever they were locked in, but though Goa was now shut down entirely on our exit, the North was still free, and relatively Covid free, at that. We were so glad to be in the arms of Himachal at last. We rose early once more, to take our final drive to Dharamshala, our imagined sanctuary.

It was not to be. Ullu had had enough; her Indian 'quick fixes' by the original mechanic had been holding her together but doing so many miles after being left dormant for some time in the Goan humidity and heat was testing her old heart. She finally let go on a steep hill as her tappet rod snapped in two and the power to push the engine any further was lacking. I was a little way behind John and as I pulled her over to the roadside, a man offered to help find a garage that might fix Ullu.

He zoomed off on his Hero Honda and returned within ten minutes promising to bring the mechanic. True to his word, a teenager on a half-dismantled scooter soon showed, but his face showed quickly that we would not be going anywhere fast. He wedged something into the crack, and Ullu kick started again reluctantly. I was told to hold her under forty miles per hour, and not to let out her clutch once when idling, to coast on the down hills, and it would get me home. We waved him off and prepared for the long drive, still many kilometres to go. Two minutes later, a huge truck swerved into my path, and my inexperienced hands in second gear let out the clutch as I braked. She stalled, and we were back to square one on the side of the road.

In pandemic times, with most businesses shutting down or being forced into lockdown, parts and spares seemed to be completely unavailable for this old bike. These old villages, dealing mainly in Hero Hondas, scooters and newer twin spark Enfield engines did not even have a mechanic who knew the machine or how to fix it. We were advised to put her on a truck and take her to Bilaspur, the nearest town, who had an Enfield mechanic.

The bike parts had to be ordered, and I then had a choice whether to put Ullu on a truck to Dharamshala and hope someone there could fix her or leave with this man who did not have a computer or a smartphone and stated that the parts needed to be collected from Chandigarh, a city some kilometres away, which could take weeks. At this point we were already a day over our scheduled arrival and getting increasingly nervous about arriving at Dharamshala and finding a place to spend the mountain lockdown. Images of being locked out of Dharamshala clouded our judgement, and we allowed the man to keep the bike, gave him five thousand rupees for the spares and work, and decided to hedge our bets. The work was worth much less, but we were in a real bind. We divided the luggage, and the fruit seller next door offered us a space under his potatoes to store our bags.

I very sadly threw my leg over the back of Pushkarini, glanced back at Ullu, and clasped my hands around his waist as we sped off.

My bike had not made it all the way, after all. I had wanted and expected to arrive roaring up that mountain path, having completed my first ever long drive on my battered old bike, proving something to someone. I did not know at the time, but the person I was trying to prove something to, was myself. India was still teaching me lessons; this was about the journey, not the destination. We had handled the busy Delhi streets, had two breakdowns, and escaped being locked down in the heat. We had done something incredible, but my ego was too bruised to see it.

As we thundered up those last few hills from Dharamsala to Mcleod Ganj town to picturesque little Dharamkot, my eyes started again to sparkle with joy. A storm had come, and as we raced up the steep little inclines to avoid the battering rain, I felt like a fairy in a children's story book, as twinkling lights from the tiny houses spread out across the hills and valleys, my heart soared as I smelt the air, scented with pine. I saw the thick green trees, and felt clouds brush at my elbows, giving a mystical feel to these valleys. We were safe. We had defied all odds to get to this isolated place, ensuring our hearts and minds would not be trapped, but in the arms of nature, Tibetan prayer bells ringing in the distance, ringing the sweet sound of hope.

TEMPORARY FIXES

Ullu had been mended to the best of the mechanic's ability, his answer to her tappet issue being, "Just sell her."

I awoke each morning to the sounds of farmers working in the fields, goats bleating, eagles crying and the views of an elf-like landscape, tiny houses in the hills. Dharamshala, famously the home of the Dali Lama, was a peaceful haven after the sensory assault of Delhi.

It did not take long for the North to follow the South in a nationwide second official lockdown. The police could not reach our mountain homes up in Dharamkot and their little paths by vehicle, and perhaps they did not want to attempt to hike the many stairs that led to our community. Just as they had not followed us into the water in Rishikesh, the police here did not bother themselves with climbing steep hills to reprimand a community of hippies for ignoring the curfew. As a result, our second lockdown was blindingly easy and afforded us many freedoms as a small village, with only one occasion of being shut in a café by locals, by candlelight in complete silence, as the police passed by.

The waterfall at the top of the hill that we lived on

became a solace, and as our bodies became fitter and stronger each day from climbing and hiking, our minds turned once again to meditation, reflecting the gentle nature of the Tibetan people. I spent months there in perfect peace, by day hiking with the goat herds and the shaggy mountain dogs, and by night, dancing in the open air at one of the many concerts. There were talented people who we had been locked down with, and it had been the same in Rishikesh. The foreigners who had been trapped were not all shoeless wanderers, but were also doctors, lawyers, artists, healers, and musicians from all around the globe.

My muscles grew from climbing and my feet hardened, barefoot on the earth once more. As much as I was enjoying the femininity of the woods and grasses, the abundance of flowers and animals, forests, and fertile green land, I could feel something calling me from afar. My thirst for adventure shouted once more, the masculine side of me searching for purpose, direction, and to feel some danger, to challenge myself. There was only one thing which I knew could help me to satiate this need: my motorcycle.

After the second lockdown began to lift, I planned for some solo motorcycling once again. My first solo trip was a few weeks later, to a beautiful place called Pulga, in Parvati Valley, which was a day's drive from Dharamshala. It was known for its premium marijuana and opium, which perhaps contributed to the slow pace of the area. It was also named for the sensational Parvati River which floods the land of elfish greenery and woodland hideaways, peppered with prayer flags whipping in the wind, with houses made of wood and straw and carved with symbols and lavish curling designs.

I was halted at many places along the way because of some recent bad weather, where the cliff had crumbled. I watched, open-mouthed, as a digger threw an enormous boulder down a valley that would have been headed for the road underneath it and I saw the road fall away with it. As much as I had studied the route, I had a few worries on top of the landslides which had been predicted. I was aware of Ullu's tappet issue which could flare up at any time, and so I needed to make sure I was near some Enfield garages. As it turned out, most of these were no use at all, the resounding answer always, "This bike is a bad bike."

I got to know a real mechanic by the ones whose eyes would shine when they saw her and would wax lyrical about her engine to the whole shop, running their hands over her and looking at her the way I did.

In Mandi, a hot and humid town on the way to Manali, the owner of a tiny motorcycle repair shop turned out to have owned the very same bike model. He told me that Machismo riders always stuck together out of love for the machine. At the earlier garages, young boys, used to brand new, squeaky-clean Desert Storm Royal Enfields, would not even look. I learnt later how different these engines are, and how much they needed regular tuning to keep them in top shape.

"These machines will run for you forever," he would tell me, grinning, "...if you keep an eye on them when they start to grumble and don't ignore it."

To ignore an engine issue on a Machismo is to cause a whole heap of trouble. Her engine was an older model compared to the newer Twin Spark engines, which ran cooler than the Machismo. It was discovered that she had a long-term issue with her tappets, with a big gap which needed to be filled, meaning that they would often be at risk of moving around too much and snapping or cracking, causing the rods to move, too. The tappet rods assisted in opening the engine valves, rotating the crankshaft, helping to power the engine. Without them working together harmoniously, Ullu would not work. I could not find anyone who would guarantee a fix, which meant constant tightening of those tappets every few hundred kilometres. I was at those mechanics faster than you could say, "ticking noise". However, the issues I faced at the mechanics were not only the make and model of my bike; it was much more complicated simply because I was a woman.

Every mechanic I went to would behave the same way; refusing to meet my eyes or listen to a word, offering me chai if I would sit in the corner or stay out of the way. I did neither.

I watched and waited while they allowed men who were more important than I in front of me as though I did not know. I learnt not to smile at all, as it had most mechanics asking for my phone number. I learnt only to ask for what I needed and refuse to budge from my spot until they did exactly what I wanted.

By this point I was learning my way around the machine; unbeknown to the mechanics I had seen enough to know a bit about how the bike worked. I had been to enough of these shops to know Ullu's issues which were repetitive and always temporary fixes, as lock down was not the time for lengthy work, and parts were scarce. Due to covid lockdowns, even 19-inch wheel bearings were unavailable, and as I watched them fix my wobbly wheel with a bit of a tin can wedged in to compensate for the wrong size bearing, I couldn't help but giggle; most of the time, repairing bikes in this pandemic was akin to sticking a plaster on a broken leg.

I understood more than they thought, picking up the lingo. I began to fight back when they tried to make up jobs, fixes that I presented receipts for, issues that did not need resolving. I used my basic Hindi and watched them eagle-eyed, until I became braver and began to sit as the mechanics did, in a squat on the oil-drenched floors, shuffling ever-nearer, insisting on being included. Later, I would pass their tools, understanding the ones they needed and learning about spanner sizes. I chided the ones who tried to tighten the tappets with a sizzling hot engine as they looked at me in consternation, confused as to why I knew this. They slapped each other on the back in mirth: the white woman on the big bike was challenging them on mechanics. Even now, armed with some idea of the inner workings of my bike, it was still a big joke to them that I was trying.

About seven or eight mechanics in, things started to change. I think I had learnt enough or perhaps just grown in confidence and in speaking Hindi. They started to take notice; refusals to do what I wanted with my motorbike now rarely happened, and they now believed what I said. I knew the pricing by now, and how to argue when I was being ripped off. I had the gestures down to a tee, the noncommittal flap of the hand to say you were disinterested, the Indian head wobble from side to side to agree, and the quick little tutting noise which meant that you did not.

Finally, one group of mechanics, named Anu Motor works, in Manali, was so decent to me that I became even braver then, and asked them to show me how they took the engine apart.

I watched as they dismantled the bike, and the lead mechanic pushed a stool across the floor to me with his foot and drew me next to him. He explained everything, handled my questions, and this time when he offered me chai, we drank together on the floor, next to the bike. I felt empowered by that group of men. To be given a place on that floor meant everything, after all my fights to be seen.

EMPOWERMENT

After her adjustment in Dharamshala, Ullu was even louder. This motorcycle had been a force to be reckoned with in terms of sound; she was the loudest by far on the highways, and people always turned their heads in rural villages. I chose to cut the engine noise and coast through most of them to avoid the stares, but if I was in the mood, I must confess I quite liked it. Riding my Enfield was like galloping on a horse at full speed or rolling carelessly down a big hill; it left me breathless. I finally understood why so many of my friends drove fast cars or did extreme sports; it awakened something in me that had been sleeping, and I vowed never to let it close its eyes again.

Ullu gave me a kind of easy confidence, fearlessness, and courage unknown to me by any other source. People would ask me often if I felt safe, but the answer was always a resounding yes. Riding Ullu was like being atop a lion; I was untouchable.

There is something very powerful about riding solo as a woman. I was suddenly able to perceive the power and freedom I had in having my legs wide open. In India, many women ride side-saddle, legs closed. It was obvious from the looks of the faces waiting in traffic in the middle of a city. It was in the approving nods of the women who were riding pillion with their partners, the shocked smiles of male bikers as they rode alongside you and did a double-take. What a privilege it is as a western woman to be able to do something like that without a second thought. In India, if you want to buy something or even go to the doctor, they will ask you your father's name, as if your own is not enough. I recognise now, living in a country that is not my own, how meaningful it is to be a female driver, how many women would jump at a chance for such freedoms, even if the core of me yearns for a day when no one will bat an eyelid at such a thing.

Ullu was becoming a dream to ride. The roar and then the steady purring of the engine, the smooth gliding out of first gear, the comfortable couch-like seat, the chrome, and the easy transition through the gears that became second nature so quickly. Taking her up difficult mountain passes, feeling the power and adrenaline flowing through my very veins. Standing on the pedals and closing my eyes on the flat, feeling like a bird in flight. Sometimes I would lean over her engine at the end of a long drive and hear it ticking as it cooled, and she felt completely alive to me, like an animal panting.

Up a particularly difficult hill, Ullu was struggling a bit, in need of some oil and a good rest for the night. A white Maruti Suzuki, the bane of my life, passed me, with screaming noises coming out of the window. To my surprise, they rode alongside me all the way up the steep bend, sticking their thumbs up and chanting, until we all reached the top.

"Keep going," they shouted, a family of about eleven all squished into this one vehicle. They smiled and waved and sped off ahead. This support continued all the way on my trip, with people cheering me on up the steep hills, and shouting words of encouragement at me over the complex ground.

To be a woman on a bike is empowering, but to be empowered back is the best feeling in the world. In a world where women just want to be treated as equals, when men consciously and unconsciously make room for women in a world still ruled by men, that makes a difference. I realised that there were allies on the roads, even in the form of Maruti Suzukis, and they gave me hope.

SOLO

As rain patters on windows with curtains squeezed shut against the morning, your eyes are the same, closed tightly, afraid to open, because you know that when morning breaks, we will have to face it.

As we lie here, my heart is like a heavy iron-clad box; it feels like someone has welded it shut, and it will not budge. It will not yield.

As your lips press mine like the softest silk, I inhale you, your beard scratching at my cheek, hands grasping at the nape of my neck. As you turn, I close my eyes to see you silhouetted; an outline of the man I have loved against a sunlit doorway, etched onto my eyes and now my mind, forever.

The goodbye came like we knew it would, soft and sweet and with heavy longing for each other, and you unable to leave, muttering sweet nothings and reaching over and over for the kiss we know could be the last. You call me your Queen, standing with your hand on your chest, your eyes grey like the heavy stone you give me, in

the shape of a heart. Mine will continue to beat for you, and I will
hold you in sleep, my fingertips brushing yours, legs entwined,
sinking deeply into your arms. When I need to, I will remember
your breath on my neck at kitchen counter tops, where water heats
for strong coffee, as we head back to bed.

I travelled the two days to Manali, with most of the scenery punctured by his face, and the slamming of memories of the two of us crossing in front of my eyes like spectres so that I had to blink them away.

John was leaving for his homeland in one month to South Africa. Trying our best not to fall apart, we had said our goodbyes early and packed our separate motorcycles for the solo trips that we had both dreamed of taking.

Our relationship had been one big lesson in non attachment, and this made us both grateful for every moment. Like the mangoes of India, we both knew that this was only ever meant to last for so long. If our love was strong enough, it would bide its time, until our season came again.

My route was spectacular, with rough road, pinecones the size of my head which blocked the road and curious mongooses slinking across my path. It was a bittersweet ride, with the throttle sometimes proving an outlet for the anger I held inside. As Ullu roared, so did I.

I reached Vashisht and threw myself into the hot springs, trying to wash away the grime of the road and the severe loneliness of the last two days. If this trip wanted to break me entirely, I was ready for it. I had left behind all that I knew and that made sense to me. I had faced death, looked a snake in the eyes, almost been impaled, and now I had lost the love of my life; it had all been a great surrender. I was about to surrender myself now to those towering, snow-capped mountains, to the dangers of another ride, and I wondered what I would find.

Leh Khardung la Pass

Thiksey

Karu

Upshi

Tanglang La Pass

More Plains

Pang

Lachulung La Pass

Sarchu

Zing Zing Bar

Baralacha La Pass

Darcha Jispa

Tandi

Keylong Chandratal Lake

Atal Tunnel

Vashisht Manali

0   10   20   40 Miles

MOUNTAINS

I set off one morning to bitterly cold skies, wearing multiple layers and two sets of gloves, on the road from Manali to Jispa. I had initially planned on going solo, but I picked up an old friend from lockdown, Laul, in Manali. We were both recently broken-hearted and both in that frightening and delicious state of connecting back to ourselves and decided that having a friend would do us both the world of good.

Laul was hardy, positive-minded, and up for an adventure. After her promise to practice jumping off at a moment's notice in preparation for those inclines we knew we would face, we waited for the correct weather to start our journey. One pass had already shut due to the weather, the famous Rohtang, which in Hindi, meant, 'ground of corpses' owing to the number of people who had died on it, and we were now forced to go through the newly- built Atal Tunnel, which was a speedier and safer way through the mountain.

We had spent a week in a threadbare guest house in Manali with thin blankets and torrential rain hammering at the windows. We were waiting for news about the recent landslide that was on our route, practising patience and grateful that we had not left earlier; a bridge was completely closed off with videos of mountainsides collapsing all over the news. The danger of the journey we were about to take was on every traveller's lips in Vashisht, with stories reaching us of riders being forced to spend the night trapped on the road.

Monsoon was not the right time of year to be crossing mountain paths, never mind with a pillion, with landslides, skimming stones and river crossings all at their highest risk at this time, and I had originally aimed for September, when it would be much less hazardous. There was no going back now; I was determined to relight the fire in me that had dwindled somehow, which I knew would come back to me in moments of survival.

"Stand your own ground, on your own two feet. Do not wait for someone to come along to protect you." - Gagori

As we said our goodbyes to Manali, we started to climb. The Atal Tunnel did not permit you to go through it with spare petrol, and so I had taken two empty large five litre containers and strapped them to the back of Ullu to be filled on the other side. As the last fuel garage for 340 kilometres, the pump at Tandi was essential. We were not going far; Jispa, we had read, would be a good place to acclimatise for the mountain passes; at 11,000 feet, it would ensure at least one good night's sleep before the chadar tents, which were the famous and temporary overnight lodgings of Pang or Sarchu, and we thought we might at least get some garam pani, hot water.

As it was, when we arrived, we got neither. The jump in

altitude made for strange, wakeful dreams, and the shower was inoperable. As we packed and re-packed the bike and stared out in wonder at the impressive mountain range in the distance, we checked our phones for a hint of Wi-Fi. No such luck. This was it; we were on our own, and we were thrilled to be. We looked at our ten gallons of petrol in cheap plastic containers and hoped that it would be enough; with no mechanics or garages in the mountains, we prayed that they would not burst, along with Ullu's tyres, on the treacherous roads.

The morning came, and we set off at six. Trucks were already roaring to life outside our window, shooting off up the pass, but we had not yet seen the convoys of army trucks. This was a good sign that we still had the roads to ourselves. Hurriedly, we jumped aboard Ullu and after a good twenty minutes of running in neutral with the choke out, she responded in the cold air, and we were off.

The route between Jispa and Pang was beautiful, non-eventful and desolate, save for a large river crossing and a large bump that displaced Laul. It was the kind of road that you find at the tops of high mountain passes, with sparse patches of colour, becoming less lush in vegetation and consisting of mainly rocks. The views, however, as you climbed higher and higher, were never-ending, with new mountain peaks appearing the higher that you go, and the vast valleys in between providing watercolour streaks of colour below.

We hit a stretch of road which had started to get a little trickier in terms of steering, as it was broken to pieces, perhaps by the many military trucks which frequented the route. As it happened, we had bumped into some friends on the route who were on a 500 engine and so had sped ahead, our speeds incomparable. They were waiting for us at the other side of this first Nullah, or river crossing, and thank goodness that they were. It took three of us to get Ullu across this first crossing, her tyres digging into the soft sandy pebbles and sinking ever lower. Water came over my rubber boots as I dug my own feet in, my bum off the seat, revving her engine, the temperature of the icy water taking my breath away. With a huge lurch, she became free of the sinking-sand effect, and the other two rocked her and pushed from behind, towards freedom. This was our first Nullah, and it would not be the last.

We arrived at Zing Zing Bar, the base of Baralacha La Pass at over 14,000 feet high and rested with an enormous convoy of military trucks who stared at us like we were extra-terrestrials as soon as we took off our helmets but smiled and waved. We experienced our first roadside chadar tent, one of five or so similar, kitted out with about twenty futon beds under a simple tarpaulin, with a steaming pot of something bubbling on the metal burners in the middle. It smelt incredible, of curry powder and toasted spices.

"Thoda thanda," we laughed to the owner, who shivered and agreed. It was cold indeed. We gratefully kicked off our shoes and shut our eyes for ten minutes, aware that we did not have long to complete the day's ride to Pang. The Ladakhi owner was very happy to see two women on a motorcycle and asked us many questions. I excused myself to use the facilities and found that the toilet was an open pit with a sheet of scrap metal for privacy, and faced the mountains, providing what might be the most beautiful bathroom view I have ever experienced.

The bump that almost caused Laul to go careering over the steep edge of the pass was so expertly hidden by the uneven nature of the road that it was only when I saw the other Enfield fly high into the air before me that I knew to expect it. I slowed, but it didn't matter. Laul had become so confident in my driving ability that she was taking photographs and was not holding on. That, coupled with the height of Ullu's custom foam seat, did not give her a hope in hell of staying put. She flew past my shoulder and came off at a great height, tumbling dramatically onto the gravel at speed. So great was the bump that she missed me entirely, and she did not grab me as she fell, or we both would have floored it. We looked back at the drop; perhaps half of my wheel height, it was a sheer drop for no apparent reason, and would probably never be fixed.

I stuck a large stone in the centre of it so that it would not unseat any more travellers and patched up Laul's wounded hand. We rode the rest of the way a little more cautiously. Friends of ours had broken their collarbones whilst crashing into cows on flat roads- there were no cows in sight, but we were, it seemed, on our way to the very top of the world and were instantly reminded of our fragility as humans and new riders. We needed our energy for Baralacha La, La meaning pass, as climbing any altitude above 8000 feet could cause altitude sickness. Sleeping at high altitudes could be life threatening, as could climbing too quickly.

We climbed the peak of Baralacha – La at 15,912 feet, which was the first time that I was hit badly with altitude sickness. We had climbed an elevation of over 4000 feet in only a few hours, the hardest part of crossing over the mountains to Leh being that there was no other option other than to risk it. We had been warned about altitude sickness; many travellers had been hospitalised in Leh or Manali due to climbing too quickly. Feeling confused, nauseous, and dizzy, I dismounted the bike and sat awhile on the teetering edge in the small space next to the bike. We chewed garlic and ginger and a bit of colour came back into our cheeks. We wobbled off, determined to get to Sarchu.

Laul and I hit Sarchu in good time for a quick chai. At about 14,500 feet, it is another resting ground for weary travellers. We had achieved 220 kilometres so far from Manali and our thoughts turned to the rules that we had been lectured by many a cadet, that we should not attempt to ride from Sarchu to Pang after mid-afternoon. We checked the time. It was two o'clock, and so we decided to risk it and push on to the next and final stop, Pang.

We started to climb the Gata Loops on the Nakee La, a series of twenty-one or so exciting uphill hairpin bends which reach an altitude of 15,547 feet at the top. It was a challenge for Ullu who had not yet had her carburettor jet changed to a smaller one. I cursed at my inability to ask the last mechanic for what I knew I had needed, as I stood up on the front pedals and leant far over the engine, switching the heavy cans of petrol to hang from the front crash-guard to balance the weight as the incline had us climbing at a pitiful speed. My passenger screamed words of encouragement as our bike complained and sputtered but refused to stop. Sometimes we hit gravel, and the combination of the incline and the weight made the bike slide, quickly and dangerously backwards, but Laul was ready for it and she expertly slid off to grasp the back of the cage to help push us up, which was no mean feat at that altitude.

The next pass, Lachlang-La, was a whopping 16,600 feet in altitude, and by this time, Ullu had developed a high-pitched engine whine, despite being given the freedom to coast down Nakee La. I went to top her up with oil and realised it had slipped out of the bag somewhere along the road. I worried for her tappets and so we went slowly, refusing to push her past a comfortable point, inching along the ascent.

I let Ullu coast down the other side, and we breathed a sigh of relief and basked in the beauty of the surroundings, rocks and greenery turning to desert once more, as we whizzed down in silence with the cooling engine, sailing past yet more army convoy trucks. We saluted them and erupted into laughter as they froze mid-wave, dumbfounded at two women on an old military bike, in welly boots and with no protective gear, hair whipping in the wind, gone again in a flash.

As we arrived in Pang, the night was just falling, and the stars were coming out; shiny white diamonds peppered across a silver sky stretching for miles. Our friends were waiting for us, boots up and waving us down on the rusty bench outside, with a small flash of whisky, wrapped in blankets against the cold air at an army pitstop. We had made it halfway.

SEXISM

My motorcycle experience has not been with trial and tribulation. As a woman traveller, I have seen my fair share of inequality and sexism off and on the motorcycle. It is worth to share these experiences, if only to point out what society already knows: we still have a long, long way to go.

'Don't gossip... let him drive.'

I would see this road sign the very next day, where road conditions had relaxed enough for a minute that the entertainment had primarily become reading these signs. Quippy and light-hearted, the Border Roads Organisation, or 'BRO', had hand-painted each of them for the travel season, the brief yearly window of June to October.

I had to stop the bike. Did my eyes deceive me or was this a blatantly sexist remark on a highway used by so many, driven past every day by truckers and workers, locals, and tourists?

I thought about all the women in those vehicles, driving or not, who would have to swallow it and say nothing. I thought of all the men who would laugh, or worse, that the phrase would not register at all. I thought of all the young girls who would see that perpetuated; the misconceptions surrounding the abilities of a woman.

Had we gone back in time?

I wrote to BRO, but I never got a response. John was so disturbed by this that when it was his turn to do this stretch of road on his solo trip a month later, he took a sharpie to vandalise several of the signs, inserting 'they' and 'them' appropriately, with big red crosses through the 'gossip' part for impact. I was told that many other travellers continued to add their thoughts as the months went on, and so who knows what it looks like now. If I must drive that road every year to make sure that sign disappears forever, I will. Gagori had told me to pick my battles, but this one had niggled at me like a licking fire in my lungs, and I knew that somehow, by refusing to shut my eyes to it, I and the other travellers were fighting it for all women.

PANG TO LEH

We woke in the early morning, and did not want to leave our rickety beds, as it was punishingly cold. No one in our party had considered showering; a bucket bath in that freezing air would have been an interesting start, and it was bad enough just splashing the cold tap water on our faces outside the chadar tent.

The 'tent' was made of corrugated iron and fabric, those famous synthetic blankets, and had a faint smell of petrol, but we had been very glad of a bed for the night. The window was made of plastic and was hanging on for dear life with the battering of the desert sand.

The auntie fixed us chai, and I made some very strong coffee for both drivers, straining the grounds through a tiny pocket sieve into a metal tureen. We did not breakfast; there was no time, the sun threatening to come up over the mountains at any moment and bringing with it the desert heat and blinding sunlight that was such an energy-zapper.

I was developing a banging headache. People had told us not to stay here, that Pang was a land of insomnia, and one could find it a struggle to breathe in the middle of the night due to the altitude of over 15,400 feet, and I found both to be true, waking up with sudden gasps at regular intervals, choking in my sleep. The same had been said about Sarchu, some 80 kilometres back along the route. With little between them in terms of altitude sickness reports, Pang had been our destination of choice, leaving fewer miles to cover on the third day as our energy depleted throughout the trip.

We loaded up our gear onto our bikes once more, which was difficult to do with gloved hands, but impossible to do without. I heard engines everywhere along the road being revved and coaxed into life by fellow travellers in huge groups; everyone in the mountains knew the rule; drive early, sleep early. Room for error in these conditions was small, these roads in the dark were perilous, and we wanted to hit the road before the truckers opened their eyes and finished their paratha. The only error that we might make which would be worse than not carrying enough petrol would be wasting it all by getting stuck behind a convoy of wide trucks, with no room to pass for miles. We knew better than to play that game by now.

Pang was like the surface of Mars. The desert changed colours around us with the rising morning sun, from gold to blood-red, to black as the mountains cast shadows on each other. It was a lonely wind that whisked through the few dhabas that lined the 'street' if it can be so-called. I felt impermanence there, as if it were a gateway to another world perhaps, and India had more up her sleeve. We were about to ride into another devastatingly gorgeous existence beyond Pang, but I could see nothing for miles except sand and rock and equally blistering cold and heat. Sometimes, to reach heavenly sights, you must work for them.

More than anything, it was deathly quiet. They say that one can go mad from silence; Pang, without the roaring of the trucks, was one of the most silent, lonely places I have ever experienced. If it were not for the warm hearts and kitchens of the Ladakhi people who came to feed the road users for those few short months that the passes were open, I would never have proclaimed it habitable.

I gave Ullu some much needed maintenance; after a wipe-down to remove the clinging sand, I procured some oil for her engine and gave her a good spray of chain lubricator. As I was finding with my fantastic machine, she was much more fuel-efficient than the bikes of my friends and still had half a tank after two hundred kilometres, possibly also due to my tendency to give my old bike as much engine relief as I could by coasting whenever possible.

I filled Ullu to the brim with about six or seven litres of petrol and threw the rest to my friend behind me who was running low on his own, praying we would make it to Leh, knowing we had passes to climb and much heat to battle through before we would come in to Leh, Ladakh at 11,550 feet.

So far, I think I had survived on snickers bars, garlic, coffee, and ginger. The high altitude had done something strange to my appetite and I found that I could not eat, so one mouthful of dal and chawal, or lentils and rice, made by a kind auntie the night before had given me the boost I needed, and as I revved Ullu up and pushed her choke back in against the cold morning air, I could feel that her top-up of oil had also invigorated her. We were ready and I had all the energy of someone who wants to see the world, knowing that what I had already been lucky enough to witness was in all honesty, out of this one. As my friend eased into the space between our luggage on the back of me and I adjusted my fully-scarved face under my helmet, we set out against the chill in the direction of that rising sun.

We hit sand dunes. After a brief argument with a

construction worker who blocked our path to what resembled a road, we were waved off in the general direction of a sea of beige. Vast and deep, it looked like terrific riding, if I was aboard a light and nimble dirt bike, with no luggage and no other souls to be responsible for.

From the moment our tyres settled into the sand and were submerged up to the mudguards, we knew that it would not be easy going. We struggled on for about forty minutes, arms braced against the wobbling handlebars, as sand brushed every inch of our bodies and Ullu's wheels sank ever lower. Somehow, she made it through, her tyres settling into tiny grooves made by previous riders which were impossible to see in the wind, causing sandstorms so great that we could only shut our eyes in defence.

We rode like that for some time, in complete trust, eyes slammed shut and riding at about thirty miles an hour, gripping hard, using our feet to steady us when we slipped. Both of us had expected to come off at any time, and we were ready for a crash.

The sand shifted so much that there was no clear path even when visibility returned, and the great storms of sand behind us shot up in the air. The path made by others was a serpentine through the bath of sand, and it became clear that all riders who had taken it were as unbalanced as we were.

When we finally hit some pebbles and Ullu's wheels found grip, I stopped, bent over the front of the bike, and allowed the lactic acid in my forearms to dissipate. I wept in gratitude, laughing, as my pillion smacked me on the back in disbelief. I made a mental note to find an alternative route on the way back; the harsh deserts of Pang having made more than an impression on me.

As we left the treacherous sand, I had no idea of what to expect next. No-one had been able to prepare us for this journey because we did not know anyone personally who had attempted it. We had not been ready for the sand, and yet here we were on the other side of it. I felt invincible. Ullu was drowning in sand, and as we wiped her clean of as much of it as we can, we realised we had both swallowed a lot ourselves.

It was burning heat, and as much as I wanted to rest my bike, we had to find some sort of shade first. There was none, as we hit more broken road mixed with dangerous bits of metal and brick. There was nothing for miles around, should we need assistance.

We sat at the side of the road with scarves over our heads, poured electrolyte crystals into the one bottle of water that we had left, and gave Ullu a valuable twenty minutes to cool down.

Ullu sounded better after a rest. We coasted luxuriously, enjoying the views. The road ahead changed again, as if someone had painted over the sky and road, and rubbed it all out, replacing it with entirely fresh artwork once more. I was spellbound. I could only liken it to Montana in the United States, with the mountains on all sides. The road was named 'More Plains'. It was a flat plateau surrounded by mountains on all sides, with a smooth road running through the length of it, with luscious green fields and picture-perfect white marshmallow clouds in a powder-blue sky. It looked like something out of a dream and would have suited an expensive car commercial – wild horses galloped alongside us as we opened our eyes wide in disbelief and shut them again quickly against the incoming whipping winds and dust in our eyes. The valley turned into a bottleneck, and we were rocked from side to side despite our loaded weight as the wind slammed into us at a great speed. We flattened ourselves against the engine for aerodynamics and in fear of being thrown off.

We started to climb yet another pass, and we laughed in

disbelief, as we had thought ourselves close to our next destination.

"This is the last one," I said aloud to both Laul and the bike, as we were beginning to tire. We longed for another coffee, but there were few tents open in this post-monsoon season as the usual number of tourists had not come through. When we got to the top, we were amazed to see white 4x4's as far as the eye could see, as now that the weather had improved, the Indian tourists who had been stuck in Leh for the landslides were returning with their local Ladakhi drivers to Manali. We had been so fortunate to have had all five high-altitude passes to ourselves without dodging vehicles the entire way, sometimes riding for hours without seeing a soul. At that moment I knew we had taken our trip for granted and reminded myself what a unique opportunity we were being afforded, to travel during the pandemic. It had allowed us our nomadic Himalayan adventure that I had always dreamed of since turning the ignition key for the first time in my beloved Ullu. Not many would ever experience the Himalayas like this, and I was not about to waste a moment of it.

This final peak, Tanglang-La, was the highest pass so far at 17,480 feet, and we were treated to some snow at the peak, but due the amount of tourists, we did not want to queue for a selfie at the stone marker as we knew we were due a covid test before Leh, at the military barrier.

The landscape soon turned again from ice to sand as we wound down through the mountains, and Laul and I found ourselves in gargantuan valleys with soaring cliff faces of what appeared to be giant anthills, shaped by the weather into the rock above us, that looked like regal carvings, ancient and dominating, strange and wonderful. I told myself that this had once been a valley of Kings and Queens, for I had seen nothing else like it in my life and imagined digging for all kinds of treasures here. The valleys revealed pristine rivers of iced blue, bubbling ferociously downstream.

The valleys eventually parted, and we were astonished to see purple and pink streaks of slate running through every crevice and crack, raspberry rippled ice-cream hills that did not look real. India, once again, had managed to reveal yet another part of her that I did not even know existed. She was truly a land of extreme diversity. I smiled as I thought of all the gems she had in her grasp to show to those who dared go these routes, and I felt as if nobody would believe me if I told them, or like in some wonderful work of fiction, that we had stumbled across pure magic.

Perhaps the altitude was playing with me; I pulled over to the side of the road to find some of these pink and purple stones, but they turned dull as I held them in my hand, and did not shine as the hills did, in the brilliant light of the sun. I pocketed one anyway.

We rode in silence, sometimes gasping aloud, imagining how few people in the world had seen such beauty. We finally passed a sign that said, 'Welcome to Ladakh' and breathed out, knowing we were close.

We waved goodbye to the snow-capped mountains as they vanished, and we drove down further in altitude, towards Leh. We passed beautiful villages of Tibetan people, who, as Ullu thundered through, turned to wave, and smile. We rested at a dhaba and accidentally found our friends, who had soared ahead on those hills.

Brilliantly, we had ended up only ten minutes behind them, as Ullu's fantastic handling had allowed us to make up a lot of time on the downhill slopes as we flew down, enjoying every curve. I had to sit awhile for the motion in my whole body to slow down and feel steady again, but those tarmac roads, after many hours of navigating hours of difficult road, were as welcome as the plate of Tibetan Thukpa noodles before me. We passed the military barrier, a simple rope and a couple of officers with those enormous ledger books and crawled our last twenty kilometres of our route.

As the roads changed and more vehicles joined us, we saw the outlined monasteries against the skyline and raced on, in the impending darkness, desperate for a comfortable bed and to wipe the grit from our eyes.

I had longed for some time to spend the night at a Buddhist Monastery, desperate to learn about the culture and believing wholly in the enormous healing power of chanting and sound vibration in such historical and gorgeous spaces. I don't know how I knew, but I felt that Thiksey, outside Leh, would have room for us, and as Ullu spluttered and coughed along the very last part of our drive, up the huge driveway leading to the most majestic and incredible looking collection of tiny white houses and Tibetan architecture, I could not shake the feeling that I was coming home.

We parked and I thanked her, kissing her fuel tank, and giving her a much-deserved pat. Tibetan monks chuckled at me as they passed me still astride her, cuddling her in gratitude, and gave me a thumbs-up and joyful shouts of, "Julley!"

"Julley!" we cried back the Ladakhi phrase meaning hello, goodbye or thank you, ecstatic at such a warm welcome.

One elderly monk came over to feel the bike and told us that he had once owned a similar model, only with no self-starter, and I giggled at the image. We had made it to Ladakh, near the border of Tibet, Ullu was a champion, and my only slightly sore companion was also in one piece. I was so tired that I could barely unpack the bike and was quite shell-shocked and in awe of our journey. What had seemed a feat so enormous had been a wonderful adventure, and now it was time to ring the stunning prayer bells, kick off my shoes, and walk barefoot up the many steps to the main temple, to give some very sincere thanks for this weary but strong body, my overheating but loyal bike, my sleepy but ever-trusting pal, and the dangerous but unbelievable landscape.

PEACE

Morning came like a hangover, quickly and without mercy. Sunlight streamed through the blinds as I wriggled into some long-sleeved clothes suitable for a temple visit, rubbed the sleep from my eyes, stretched out my back after sleeping on the hard boards and heaved myself up the steps once more. I had heard that the monks chanted in the mornings here, and I was not about to miss what I knew would be something I would never forget.

As I stepped over the threshold, there was no one else in the monastery but for the low sounds of the monks in the temple above, the sound of gongs being struck, and the gentle whistling wind. I silently padded across a peaceful courtyard and ran my hand along the backs of two lion statues that welcomed me in. I climbed the steps to the entrance and was suddenly shy; the reverence I felt as a white foreigner attempting to enter such a space was overwhelming. I need not have worried; as I bowed my head with hands clasped together and shuffled inside slowly so as not to distract the rows of red-robed monks, I received a gummy smile and a little wave from an elder monk to direct me to the back, where cushions and low lighting promised to be a most comfortable viewpoint.

The walls were cool and the whole hall smelt dusty, of ghee and candle wax. I sat there for a long time, breathing in and out, feeling the thin fabric underneath me covering the wooden boards where I sat, in stillness. The combination of tiredness and gratitude had made me so emotional that I began to feel tears escaping my eyes and rolling down my cheeks. I took huge gulps of air that was heavy with spirit and intention and listened to the monks as they chanted.

I do not know how much time passed, and then, as with all the most wonderful experiences, suddenly it was over too soon. I opened my eyes to find only a few monks remaining, running their hands over scriptures and others dutifully refolding, tidying. A tiny monk held a huge kettle which I later learnt was full of Po Cha butter tea, a staple of each monastery I would visit, tasting a little bit different every time.

The heavy wooden door frame, adorned with simple fabric hangings in vermillion, marigold, and jasmine, leads the way into a Great Hall in which twenty monks are chanting. Little ones sit impatiently, rocking back and forth, and rearranging their robes, cushions, and scriptures. Each has a mentor to guide them alongside, and as they fall against their elders in tired frustration, their brotherhood is clear. As they lift their instruments, they are practiced in their art, their earlier japes in stark contrast to their concentration and devotion. It is cleverly done, for each plays a part in the morning, and is given a part to lead, but there is no ego here, only a strong sense of togetherness.

The hall is ranked in experience; the strongest singers are grouped, and voices soar above horns and trumpets, cymbals, and bells. The eldest of the monks sit together, their chants barely whispers, their peace palpable, and they hardly move at all. Some are completely still, except for the movement of their lips, and their chests rising and falling.

The learned stand out; a boy of about nine years sits next to a microphone and his chants are audible; he knows every word without consulting his book. Occasionally they walk about, dipping out of the hall to lie in the sun, and stretch. A small monk tips a glass of water over the head of a peer; their antics bring me joy. The elders do not discipline them but smile softly, and the little ones scuttle back to the hall, to continue their prayers.

As two monks with horns ascend to the rooftop, the sound rings out across the skies; this is a celebration, the beginning of the day. As the prayers close, some hours after they first started, the air is completely silent, but vibrations continue to ring out across the monastery and prayer flags rustle in the gentle breeze.

It is done now, and tiny monks in red robes hurry to carry piping hot tea in simple silver kettles down winding steps, towards the breakfast hall, where they will break their fast.
Over the parapet, mountains surround the walls on every side, purply pink in the early light. A carpet of green at its feet, and banked in the sand, the place is awash with every colour, a joy to the eyes. Snow starts to appear at the furthest edges, as white clouds puncture the picture-perfect blue skies, and the entire valley slowly rubs its eyes and awakens too.

I squinted my eyes against the bright sun behind the heavy temple door, gave my whispered thanks to one of the singers who was now apparently sleeping bolt upright, and felt the harsh mountain rays on my skin as I stepped out into the upper courtyard, that view. On all sides were mountains, thunderously dark, with spiky ridges as far as the eye could see, like the back of a sleeping dragon.

I could suddenly see exactly what we had achieved in those three days. As the highest point for miles, Thiksey Monastery and its view did not disappoint, and as eagles soared in the wind above, the fabric on the brass whipped ferociously and fought the battering wind, as I looked down the mountainside over the parapet, towards Leh.

NUBRA VALLEY

We carried on further, through Leh, a dry desert city and joint capital of Ladakh. I had heard about one monastery named Diskit, and to get to it we would have to ride over the mighty Khardung La, famously known as the world's highest motorable pass, at 18,600 feet. BRO discovers and build new passes all the time, but for the year that we attempted this trip, locals had said that this was the one to beat. Of course, this made up my mind, the allure of a tricky road too delicious to ignore.

The pass itself was a breeze, though very high. Ullu and I were talking the same language now, and I knew exactly how far I could push her. I had finally adjusted her carburettor in Leh, and she was now galloping up hills. We had knocked all the sand and dust out of her air filter and given her a wash down with a strong hose which had revealed buckets of sand in every available crevice. It was incredible to witness her prowess on the paths now that she was equipped for it, and I was taking advantage of her new stamina.

Not far up the pass, the weather turned savage. The rain beat down on us, soaking into every edge of our clothing, as we rode away as quickly as we could to escape the rain-clouds. At the peak, we were surprised to see thick ice and snow, and suddenly we realised how cold we were becoming. We took a few minutes to high five at the top and to admire the great glaciers which towered above us. I lost a glove somewhere and was concentrating so hard on the road that when we got to the bottom, my hand was purple and almost frozen into a claw with the cold. We made it to Diskit and spent all our money on a room with a big bed and access to hot water, with somewhere to dry our drenched belongings and to sleep.

Diskit Monastery was the home of an enormous gold Buddha statue that was as elegant as it was imposing. We stayed there for sunset, admiring the typical poplar trees of Ladakh in the distance and the multicoloured mountains, some blanketed in snow and others dry as a bone, as crimson as the fading sun behind them.

In the morning, we shuffled out of bed and climbed the many stairs straight into a tiny room at the top of the monastery, where the monks could be heard praying. There were far less monks, but they had been there for many years, and were all extremely old. Despite their age, their morning chanting, which we had made it just in time to experience, was hauntingly beautiful. The low bass notes of the monks created a strong sound, vibrating through my chest and anchoring me into position so that I was unable to move until they were finished. I had learnt to sit, after all. I am unsure if it was their age or their technical prowess, but the vibrations were powerful, and seemed to hit every bone in my body, every beam in the low-ceilinged and dusty room, until I could feel it in my teeth, my fingertips, my eyelids, and each strand of my hair. I was alive with the electricity of their voices, and I began to think about the power of sound.

Buddhist chants such as 'Om Mani Padme Hum' are

powerful phrases which, when repeated, are said to gather a certain emptiness within us, which helps to detach from thoughts, emotions, and desires, to help us focus on inner peace and awareness, and, in this way, remove all our suffering. If Hinduism is learning to understand the soul, then Buddhism is separating from it, and both are concerned with the search for peace, in beautifully different ways.

As I opened my eyes in the silence after the chanting, I was drunk with peace, my body sluggish with relaxation, as if I had been massaged for hours. Then the energy came, and I felt as if I had slept for days, renewed.

A monk placed a cup in my hand. Their butter tea was different again, this time oily and saltier than Thiksey Monastery, and served with a simple roti. As I sat in the tower room sipping, in the aftermath of the prayers, I contemplated the delights and possibilities of living in a monastery in the sky forever. I was shaken back to reality by the whistling wind through the windowpane; we had more adventures ahead of us, and not much time to get there.

We were headed home again, with the promise of many a tired biker for me to be able to massage, the allure of paid work in difficult times too great to ignore. If I left it too late, there would be no travellers coming down the passes at all, and I would be penniless. Our trip, though laughably cheap by Western standards, had taken me quite some time to save for.

After making it back to our favourite monks at Thiksey, we were given a huge plate of food, sitting with the monks on one long table. After asking our fill of questions about their culture and spending one more night in the silence of the Monastery, we packed our bags full of muddy clothing onto Ullu and prepared ourselves mentally for the journey back. We were about to do it all again, backwards.

We set off at six o'clock in the morning towards Manali,

but we had one more stop head of us, the famous Tso, or Lake, named Pangong, which was hailed as impossible to miss on any trip to Ladakh. After hours of steady and unin-terrupted driving, we stopped for a chai at a dhaba and Ullu would not start again. We were high up on a mountain pass, and she needed a kick start. She had been serviced in Leh, and had had an oil change, so I was quite sure that the issue was the altitude. I put her on the middle stand and prepared to mount her again, my foot poised to kick.

"Your bike is not good. You should not have come here with this bike." A passer-by said, clothed from head to toe in the most expensive gear, pads and jacket and a go-pro camera sticking out of the side of a pristine white helmet, the tag hanging off his collar and his own bike still covered in factory plastic. He then gestured to the choke on the side.

"There is this thing called a choke..." he began to mansplain, loudly, in front of a huge table of bikers.

"...I know what a choke is." I cut him off loudly, with all the confidence that I could muster in such brash company. I sucked my teeth, such an Indian response.

I realised that no matter how competent I felt, I might still be viewed as inexperienced, less confident, incapable, and weaker by someone who had just that week rented the latest expensive model from a tour company, their mechanic riding in the back of the jeep to support them should their tyre pop. They didn't know what it had taken for me to cross this land, or anything about me, my journey, or my bike.

I realised that it was expected that I would not know. Those assumptions are made by those who shout, "kick stand" before I set off, even though it is the last move I make, even though something as simple as that should not be enough to make my blood boil in frustration. I took a deep breath, as did Laul.

"This bike is the best bike," Laul said to the man, sweetly.

I prayed the redness in my face did not show, or the whites of my angry knuckles, as I gripped my handlebars a little too hard, kicked and coaxed her thunderous engine into life, and we laughed with satisfaction as I revved her up against the cold air, and let the roadside cafe full of bikers hear her roar.

PANGONG TSO

India's magic wand had conjured up many spectacles so far for this trip, but the blue lake of Pangong will remain one of the most astonishing sights I have ever seen. The water of the majestic lake was so bright that I had to blink; I did not know that this colour existed in real life, and it took my breath away.

Pebbled beaches banked the water which rippled in the wind, and Indian tourists, finally free of their locked down cities, flocked to the tents which lined the bank. They shivered in their leather jackets, most unprepared for the cold of Ladakh outside their plastic-covered, rented SUVs, now hurriedly being scrubbed free of the mud by the staff. Laul and I bargained with a female tent seller and managed to get the hefty price of 2,000 rupees down to half price for the night, enabling us to stay to see the sunset. Indian women were always very kind to us, a sisterhood instantly formed, a bond which we did not need to ask for, but which was always apparent. It was comforting to see a woman managing a business surrounded by so many men in the middle of nowhere and so we made a beeline for her place. It was already minus in temperature at four o'clock in the afternoon, with great gusts shaking the poles that held the tents together.

I skipped a stone across the vast water to make sure that it was real and sat down to meditate. As I looked up at the mountains which surrounded the lake, it was impossible to believe that I was still in India. Pangong Tso was 14,270 feet high in altitude, and its length spanned from Ladakh into China and Tibet. It was shared between them, a lake under much political contention, like their borders. Prayer flags whipped in the blisteringly cold air, the water reflecting the tall mountains in an upside-down mirror, the tell-tale dark Ladakhi rocks under our feet.

Gales blew through the tent all night and the power went out after dinner, a simple dal. Though we were wrapped in thick blankets, we shivered all night. The tent next to us turned out to be a group of Indian men who had procured some whisky and were celebrating something loudly, Punjabi songs ringing out into the night, interrupted by the howling wind. Our wet shoes were still dripping when the morning came, and it took several tries to start Ullu, the cold biting her engine as it did our faces.

The road home, in the dark before sunrise, was one of the hardest routes I have taken aboard Ullu, mainly because we had no electricity to make coffee for the drive and neither of us had slept in the altitude and with the whisky-fuelled party next door. The name of the pass back to the Manali Leh road was Chang La, and only on our return did we hear other reviews from other bikers about the 17,688 feet high pass, which was bouldered and hard going with such a heavy load. Laul had lost feeling in her hands from having to hold on so tightly as we bounced from rock to rock, muscles aching from the strain of staying on, and my bones felt as if they would rattle out of their sockets. The combined humans, petrol, two bags and motorbike weight, lack of sleep, and days of careful driving had exhausted me. Riding in the mountains was not to be underestimated, and the reason why people prepare for it so well.

We stayed the night in Sarchu, the only other desert camp, and were so sore from riding that it was hard to make up our bunks. We had run out of money halfway there and were debating asking the military to take us in, having no choice but to choose between lunch and lodgings, when a kind stranger offered some money so we could have a bed for the night. The camaraderie we had experienced on the road was never more apparent than at that moment.

The Indian Himalayas is full of the most practical and generous people; knowing you would not wish for anyone to be stuck in those kinds of conditions, most will go above and beyond to help each other in times of need, volunteering their own petrol, rope, tools or even a spray of chain lubricant, should anyone need it. Indian generosity is a knee-jerk reaction that is built into the culture everywhere, non-negotiable good deeds which benefits both parties, their Karma, whether they are Buddhist, Hindu, Sikh, or Jain. I witnessed many acts of kindness on these roads, seeing first-hand how survival is often teamwork.

As I tied the rope to our hut shut and awaited the whistle of the pressure cooker announcing freshly steaming dal, I looked up at the sky, at the billions of stars that spread across the black. I walked a short way into the desolate wasteland that was the Ladakhi desert and heard only the call of the wind whistling through the narrow gaps of the iron huts behind me. Ullu was already covered over in sand once more. I rubbed my hands together and hurried back inside to the warm little chadar tent.

We set off before sunrise, and reached Manali in only two days, mainly out of desperation not to spend another night at that altitude. I spent the following days in a disconnected haze after flying up and down all the passes; perhaps Ullu had picked up the scent of her favourite mechanics in Manali, or it was the change of the carburettor jet, but she had behaved like a 500cc engine, keeping her speed the whole way. We managed to escape the deep sand pits on the way back, finding instead broken sections of road which ended suddenly with half metre drops, and sharp concrete edges which could easily have nicked a tyre or two. I drove like a woman possessed, running only on coffee and garlic, and any fear of the route had vanished, as we knew exactly what we were up against, this time.

We sat in our guesthouse in Manali in shock; we had survived the trip with only minor injuries, and Ullu was still in one piece, as far as I could tell. As I waved goodbye to my pillion and dear friend as she left to sample the delights of Kasol, I knew it would not be long until the urge hit again for another expedition.

I lasted three weeks, massaging every traveller in town to save enough money for fuel, desperate to be in the wild once more. I gave Ullu a spa day in the mechanics, and myself a day in the hot springs, and then we hit the road again, this time to Spiti Valley.

VASHISHT

I lift my eyes to the curling steam above my head and gaze out at
the dusk. The water shimmers with heat, the pool a dark grey with
the fading light. The mountains are just visible; their white-topped
majesty beckons above the tiled rooftops and exquisite stone.
Though I am bare, I am not cold. As night sets in I sit and meditate,
breathing in warm wisps of breath into my lungs.

The women squat under four simple Tibetan fountains, each hotter
than the rest, and bathe their bodies with their bare hands. The
relief is palpable; the heat and the water soothing even the hardest
heart, and even the angriest of souls is tamed into submission in
moments. Women of work, with strong shoulders and hands for
carrying crops up mountain ridges, heavy baskets on their backs,
come to shake off the day and nurture their hardworking feet.

Wrinkled and elastic women catch water in plastic jugs to rinse the
soap from their grandchildren, as small-breasted foreign girls
nervously sit around the edges of the bath like statues. Mothers,
ample-breasted and keen-eyed, chide the young ones and pour

water over their sisters; a small child grabs my hand to descend the
slippery steps.

The child takes a sliver of soap and begins to wash a stranger,
carefully, and with such concentration. It is beautiful. Alive with
laughter, the line of women dissolves into mirth, hearts full of
connection; the child, or bachchi, and her unconditional love have
bridged the gap as she offers her eager, soapy hands to another. I
lift her high above my head as if she is flying, and her eyes open
wide. This tiny one invites eyes to meet meaningfully across warm
water, knowing not for one moment how great is her contribution.

Women of all colours and sizes sink into the pool, and languages of
all kinds begin to stir. I listen to flowing Hindi and Nepalese, the
tones sing-song, dancing on the stone tiles in echoes. I close my eyes
and soak in its perfection; never have I felt so close to my sisters.

Calmed and bathed of the long day, the women dress daintily,
suddenly aware of showing skin, with others holding cloth for them
to shelter behind, into traditional kurta. Embroidered shirts lift
over bare breasts, perhaps to prepare for the evening rest. As I
clothe myself in turn and walk back up the shining steps, I smile at
the women I leave behind in the pool. They do not return my
smiles; they have no more time for my interest, as backs of little
ones are scrubbed and underwear washed, wrung out and pocketed,
until the dawn breaks once more.

DISTANCE

I miss you this morning.
As silent, constant tears run down my cheeks, I am sure the wetness
has furrowed tracks into them; permanent reminders of this
pausing of my heart's fullness. My chest fills up with longing.

The pain comes and goes, sometimes like a gentle breeze ruffling
my skin; memories, beautiful reminders, dance on my soul and
turn up the edges of my mouth so that I am smiling, and grateful.
Other times, it is like tiny knives slicing at the core of me, and
running rivers of loss, of grief, into my whole being, settling and
pooling around my chest.

If I was to be in your arms, I know that I would lie there until I
took my last breath, my last beat sounding on your chest, my lips
nestled into your neck. My insides rip like velcro, so great
sometimes that I fear that all the joyful parts of me will tumble out
onto the dirt road, and I will too, and I could lie there, and wait for
the crows to come.
They can take me.

I wait for his call, his reply to me. It has been three weeks and seven hours, and I am without answers, without a clue to his heart but the telepathy of our love tells me what I do know, that like mine, it is aching.

Is this what it was like for lovers in olden times, the waiting, the suspense of it, desperate for news from the one you long for? The romance I naively believed in is misleading; it is harsher than the climate I ran to.

The urge to pour my heart out, to empty it of all its words, to tell it to my love in professions of lust and wanting. Love letters. I would send them on the feet of birds if there were no other way to reach him. I would put pen to paper, ink and envelope and stamp and waxy seal, and send it in the wind, but there is no post box, no address of him.
And yet I wait for news of his heart, to see if it still beats for me, for us, for this love that we also threw into the wind to see if it would come back to us.

SPITI VALLEY

If the roads of Ladakh were treacherous, then Spiti Valley was a long, straighter version, but ninety percent of the road from Khoksar to Kaza was not made for anything other than dirt bikes and 4x4's. I had wondered about hiring another Royal Enfield called a Himalayan. It was a powerful and nippy bike with a 411cc engine, and a tailpipe conveniently lifted for all those Nullahs. It was the motorcycle that everyone chose when exploring Spiti Valley, but it felt like cheating on Ullu, denying her an experience that I knew she had the spirit for. As I waved goodbye to the mechanics and a brand-new rented motorcycle, I was full of confidence from my trip to Ladakh, and too full of bravado to have asked about the state of the road.

It had been weeks since Ullu and I had been together, and many more nights of nursing a broken heart. The journey to Ladakh had healed me in so many ways, from the Buddhist monks and their resonant voices to the imposing, other-worldly Himalayan mountains. Now it was time to fall into the loneliness of a solo voyage, the way that I knew would be essential to my learning.

I set off before the chai wallahs opened, just as the sun was trying to push above the snowy peaks in the distance. I drove for an hour until the ground changed, and I then knew I was in the beginnings of the valley. I felt Ullu's wheels squelch and slip into the mud and stones.

The riding was excellent in that it was both difficult and scenic, as the jade green mountains of Spiti Valley began to emerge and the roads became more dishevelled. Metal spikes protruded from the path for no reason, entire pieces of clay road had slipped into the river beside me, and the way was entangled with sheep and goats at every turn. I felt her mudguard rattling on a path that was pure boulders and wondered if she would make it the whole way to Kaza. I was driving at about ten miles per hour, owing to the enormous boulders over which Ullu was having to bounce over, but the lack of speed only meant a need for greater control of the bike.

I stopped at a dhaba and met some other bikers. I watched as others had no choice but to trust their belongings to the trucks of locals bound for Kaza, as bungee ropes frayed and snapped and as various parts of other motorcycles broke apart with the unsteady road. Ladakh had been a difficult ride with many different challenges, but this road was like being on a constant bouncy castle, even with Ullu's fantastic suspension.

The roads turned from green valley to patchy earth, and then I was in desolation once more. I stopped for a while on a dirt-brown plain on which were gigantic clay boulders which seemed to have been thrown there, as if a giant had been playing marbles on a tabletop. There was no other sound but the crunching of my boots as I walked in the dirt of the desert, marvelling to myself how only minutes ago I had been riding in grassy green banks. The sun was overhead at midday and meltingly hot, as I soaked a scarf in lukewarm water and tied it around my head and sat in the scrap of shade next to a boulder. Ullu's engine needed regular breaks as it always had, and I had fought across the stones for hours, but the temperature of the day was too warm for her to cool down entirely. It was too long a drive to stop for long, however.

I was on a particularly bad section of road nearing Kunzum Pass when two riders ahead of me started to slide backwards on the sand-dusted incline at an alarming rate. Reacting quickly, I raced to catch them and their bike and sliced my hand in the process, nicked on their smashed luggage cage. The pair, decorated in arm and knee pads, survived the fall. The bikes did not; their luggage cage completely hung off, and my Ullu, hastily parked, was taken by the whipping wind, falling on her side, wrenching the clutch handle off entirely. The road had managed to break many bikes to pieces, and I was only halfway to the day's destination.

A little further down the road, I realised I had a clanging sound, identifiable by the swinging end of the exhaust, which meant the moment of heroism had knocked a nut loose, too. All hopes of arriving unscathed tarnished, I looked to the positives: a road covered edge to edge in boulders, sharp rocks, sand, and stones, without a moment of a clear path; this had truly been incredible riding. Spiti Valley was certainly living up to my expectations in terms of difficulty, and Ullu was hanging on well.

I pushed on, chasing the sunset through the overhanging cliff faces, great canyons of stone, steep-sided mountain paths and patches of deep sand, and arrived to see the first star peeking at me through the middle of two mountain peaks. I stopped then, in wonder, and watched as more appeared, in a perfectly black sky. I thought back over the terrain; riding in the clouds, devastating drops and hairpin bends and grinned to myself, replaying over my favourite moments in my mind.

Next time, I promised Ullu, *I will take a rental to such tough terrain, and spare both our backs.*

I never kept this promise as she continued to bravely soldier on for months afterwards, this classic bike with a natural knack for off-roading.

After Losar, a minuscule Tibetan village of about ten houses, the ground under Ullu's tyres finally turned into buttery-soft tarmac and resembled a road once more. I began to relax. The smoothness of the road was so soothing after hours of tense driving, and I was so tired that I allowed Ullu to coast slowly for a few minutes and shut my eyes. I sleepily snaked my way through tiny villages and farmers' fields and took deep breaths of mountain air to energise me for the remaining drive. As the stars smeared over the heavens and a silver crescent rose above, I followed the moonlight all the way to Kaza.

The next morning, I took Ullu to the one and only mechanics in Kaza and watched them fawn over her vintage shape and booming engine as they fixed her exhaust and clutch handle back on.

I am a Machismo girl through and through, I thought, as I beamed with pride at that beautiful machine and all we had achieved together so far. At that moment, if I had been offered any other bike, I would not have swapped her for all the money in the world.

THE LONGING

If I saw you now, I would fall straight back into your arms and the two of us would not surface.

Days would pass, the nights too, and we would starve in love, like martyrs, and refuse to drink naught but the nectar of the other. We would not come up for air; we would breathe only the cyclical breath of long kisses.

The stars would come out, and the moon, too, but we would not see their light. The rains would come, and fall all around us, and time, our heavy burden would be silenced and forced not to tick.

I would taste you, sweeter than the mangoes in mango season, and let your sweat dictate the smell of me, let your hands and tongue find every corner of my being, and I would kiss your feet.

THE NULLAH

I had heard about the river crossings on these Spiti Valley roads from many a biker on my travels. After hearing horror stories about the Ladakh Nullahs, I had found them to be a challenge but not frightening. Riding with a pillion also meant the fear level had decreased knowing I had someone there for a push if needed. Ullu and her weight, especially with luggage, could be a trial when hitting difficult terrain; but so far, we had always made it through without catastrophe and with only a gentle soaking.

The Nullah on the way to Chandratal Lake stands out in my mind not for the danger of the road, but as the greatest feat that I attempted solo on a motorbike. You would hear the Nullahs before you saw them; rounding a corner, the rush of water as it cascaded down the sides of the cliffs, across the stone filled roads and down the sharp drops, and many were fast-flowing and difficult to judge in depth.

In hindsight, four o'clock in the afternoon was not the time at which to attempt a river crossing, as the sun had melted ice from the mountains, and it was now rushing down onto the road. A whole morning of travel to get to the

Chandratal Lake campsite had forced me into napping in my tent, and I missed the peak time to cross.

From what I had learnt about riding early in the mountains, the water on the peaks would freeze at night, and slow the flow. By morning, it would barely cover the tires as I passed through them, but by afternoon, it was a different story altogether.

With every other Nullah, I had gotten into the habit of jumping off my bike and inspecting it to find a way through, which delayed me somewhat but was a lifesaver many times. I would watch other bikes go through the river crossings, and many times would giggle at indians in flip-flops trying to get a grip on the floor enough to push their bikes through.

On many occasions I leapt off to help, to the surprise of many men whom I can only assume thought I had dropped from the sky, based on the wideness of their eyes. They would zoom off, never thinking to help me through as well, but I did not mind as I did not ask them to. I thought I had it all in hand, until Chandratal Lake.

The lake itself was very famous, shaped like a moon that gave it its name. It was a famous spot, and I was worried that I would find hundreds of people there, as I watched 4x4's career round sharp mountain edges carrying, as usual, more than the vehicle's capacity of Indians all smushed into every available space. Watching the four-wheel drive vehicles barely make it through the water should have been indication enough, but time was pressing on, and I wanted to make it for sunset.

What I could have done was waited until a convoy came and asked them for assistance. I did not inspect this stretch of water, not knowing that it was deceptively deep. From the road, it looked straightforward enough, and I had learnt never to take the middle of it directly due to water collecting there and making it deeper. With the edge being a steep drop, I assessed that I could edge in nearer to the inner bank, and the ground might be higher, with a bit more grip. The lottery was the rocks; some hidden below the water could grab your tire at any time, and speed was needed to conquer them.

Instead of calculating a route, I looked at the time and the rushing water and decided to go for it. I lifted my feet up out of the water and revved her engine.

I gave myself a head-start down the path and barged straight into the water in first gear. I sailed across, water forcing up and over my boots and reaching my waist, until a well-placed rock stopped play entirely. Ullu lurched forwards and sideways, lodging her front tyre between two boulders.

To keep the engine going to prevent water from entering her exhaust, I held onto the accelerator for dear life as she fell dramatically into the water. I was lucky that I did not fall off, such was the bump to her front, but now both legs were submerged, my left leg bent under her with freezing mountain water at my hip. I was leaning at a forty-five-degree angle, with an engine that was threatening to drown if Ullu were to stop for even a moment.

It was not a choice. I know this now, looking back. There are reports of parents who lift cars off trapped children in emergency situations; hysterical strength, I think it is called, when the body will react in an adrenaline-filled state, to save their young. Well, I was no parent, but I would not leave her here in this fast-flowing river, although common sense informed me that I may very well soon need to do so.

Knowing that I could have hours to wait for another vehicle to pass, I stuck her in neutral, dismounted my bike completely and, between revs, used the tiny handhold on the left side which would usually assist in putting her on the middle stand, to force her up and back and away from the two rocks. This took several tries of rocking her back and forth and proved futile. Stretching my whole body across the bike I attended to the throttle, and quickly moved rocks out of her path with the other hand. I felt my obliques rip and tear as the sheer force and weight of the bike zapped more of my strength from me, and, satisfied that I had cleared my route, I took up the challenge of lifting her.

As I used up my remaining strength, a guttural sound erupted from my lungs, a war cry, and somehow, Ullu responded to my screaming muscles and began to lift. I held her against the flow of the powerful water long enough to mount her. Ullu was beginning to make stuttering noises, her tailpipe submerged, and I knew that I did not have long.

With one final deep breath, I kicked her into first and aimed her around the rocks and up the bank to the other side. I screamed as I did so, encouraging my bike to make it, and skidded to a halt on the dry gravel, collapsing over the engine for a moment and allowing tears of gratefulness to flow. I revved any last trace of water from her exhaust and heard her power resound defiantly across the mountains around me. A howl escaped from my throat, catching at my lips, the sound of freedom, achievement.

I stayed there for a minute vocalising hard at the sky, shaking my whole body free of the tension it had held for so many minutes, and laughing through my tears. That feeling will stay with me forever and further cement the bond with a bike that had brought me across India, my Ullu, who kept defying the odds and refused to quit in the most important moments, both of us stubbornly unwilling to give up on the other.

THE MUSK DEER

AN INDIAN FOLK TALE

One day a young Musk Deer lifted their head and smelled an intoxicating smell on the wind. The deer was spellbound; this was a most enticing scent. The desperate deer wandered through the forest sniffing at every tree trunk, every branch, rock, and blade of grass. Sometimes the smell would be overwhelmingly close, and other times, so faint they could barely remember it. The deer became addicted to the smell, and they decided that if they found the source of this scent, they would be profoundly happy.

The deer searched the whole world, every corner, and still, they could not find the source of the smell. As the years passed, the deer became old and one day fell to the ground, exhausted. As they did so, they curled up and one of their horns pierced their belly. Suddenly the air was full of the most beautiful scent. In their final moments of consciousness, the deer realised that what they had been searching for their entire life was something that they had carried within them all this time.

POLITICS

I left Spiti Valley, desperate to explore more of Jammu and Kashmir, a state that stretched from Leh to Spiti Valley to Srinagar. I chose to drive down through the army base of Pathankot due to the unpredictable nature of my geriatric bike. It is one thing to have courage, but another to defy good advice from my favourite mechanics, who had warned me that there would be no assistance and no lodgings if I broke down on one particularly unplottable road through Zanskar Valley.

I was never worried for my safety as a solo female traveller in India because everyone I had met on my travels in India had always been so gracious and giving. I had always been vigilant and cautious, but I now realised how naive it was, travelling solo on a military-green bike, about to enter a state where the military was so prevalent.

They were testing for Covid at the border of Jammu, but as soon as I pulled off my helmet, they waved me over to chat to them and to shake my hand. They smiled and thanked me for visiting, asking me to tell my friends of the beauty of

Jammu and Kashmir. I would later discover why they were so desperate for more tourism.

I reached the hills that separated Jammu and Kashmir in the unbearable heat of the late morning and wrapped my whole face in a scarf against the road dust. The road was hard going in the afternoon heat, with heavy construction for the entire route, with brief breaks of being held up behind a sea of goats and tiny ponies, much to my amusement. I noticed the signs on the back of the trucks changed in language from Hindi to Urdu, and smiled as I read the same message, only with different brushstrokes.

I was exhausted from the heat when the dust-clad roads finally gave way to motorways, and my surroundings grew heavy with armed military, gigantic tanks speeding past me with guns pointed in every direction, and at me as I drove. I stopped on the side of the road to put on another layer of clothing and looked up to find a gun pointed in my face. I was terrified but tried to stay calm as he spoke in a language which I did not understand. As soon as I removed my helmet to explain what I was doing, they were all smiles, clapped me on the back, and put their hands together in prayer, waving as I thundered off again, swinging their guns by their sides as they walked.

The state of Jammu and Kashmir, in the North-West, on India's border, had been fought over by both Pakistan and India. After the British rule ended, Jammu and Kashmir was given a choice to join one of the two countries, but took too long and were invaded by Pakistan. India sent troops, on the understanding that Jammu and Kashmir would remain an Indian state. Jammu and Kashmir is a Muslim-majority state and was given autonomy and independence in the 1940's as India agreed to control both defence and communications but allowed Kashmir to control many of their own affairs. This was named Article 370. It was then divided into two: both Pakistan-ruled and Indian-ruled territories.

It was meant to be a ceasefire, but has been a place of perpetual unrest, exacerbated further by the Indian government's decision to strip Jammu and Kashmir of its previous autonomy, with their proclamations that Article 370 promoted separatist ideas. Violence ensued and local communications were shut down to prevent unrest, and tourists fled, leaving locals and businesses in dire straits, as they are to this day, with the suffering economy. Travellers became too frightened of the tensions to pay a visit, hearing stories of street stonings and explosives, despite the awe-shattering beauty of the region, the generous nature of the people and some parts being labelled 'The Switzerland of India'.

The sadness that proud local Kashmiris have felt at losing their state is strong, and it is a complicated matter. It mainly concerns the Kashmiri heritage, as they fear that outsiders will buy out the land, making it a Hindu majority state and possibly eradicating their culture, while India believes it will unite them as a country.

As soon as I was over the border, I pulled in for a Kahwah tea, a green tea made with cardamom, cinnamon, saffron, and almonds, and went to pay, but my money was refused because someone had paid for me, a Muslim man wearing a skull cap, a traditional Kashmiri Khan dress and a Sadri, an embroidered waistcoat. He put his hands together in a thank you gesture.

The locals flocked to me, as they could not believe that I had come to their state alone, as a woman on a motorbike. The same happened when I tried to buy food, and locals were trying to press gifts to my hands, tokens of their beloved state. They openly cried when I said I would return. They told me they prayed to Allah every day for peace, so that their children would know a safe home. Despite the tensions and politics of the state, and the military guns I was not used to, from the minute that I set foot over the border of Kashmir, I felt only the outpouring of love from those people and their deep pride for their home.

RECONNECTION

John and I met after months apart on the edge of the famous Dal Lake, as I pulled off my helmet and grinned at him. He held his arms out open wide and flashed his dashing smile.

We had rekindled our love, finding little peace without the other but growing in self. We had dreamed of journeying in the Himalayas together and it had seemed to both of us that one last motorcycle adventure with each other should be on the cards. Before his final departure to his homeland, we had decided to team up and explore some of the most dangerous passes that we could find, for one last, memorable journey. While John had camped his way back from Leh across an upper route via Kargil and near Pakistan, I had ducked under the opposite way. I fell into his arms as if I had never left them, and parked Ullu next to Pushkarini once again.

We slept aboard a traditional houseboat, with tapestries on the walls, the romance of the waterlilies and shikara boats allowing for long luxurious days reading fiction on the water and attending to each other. We rode through Srinagar, wide-eyed with wonder at the Mughal architecture and the colourful mix of Hindu and Muslim culture living so close together.

I watched him driving on Pushkarini. The mountains had always suited him, in a wool jumper, thick boots and jeans and a beard that he had let grow a little longer than before. I had known him in Goa, sculpted and shirtless in only a threadbare pair of shorts and bare feet, but my lover was most impressive to me when I watched him in the wilderness. His smell was an intoxicating mix of cold air, engine oil, and tobacco as he stopped to kiss me against the bike, his hands in my hair.

We drove for hours, stopping only for the odd banana or to fill our water containers from a stream. We decided to sleep next to a river and headed to the picturesque Aru Valley. We drove through the forests of Kishtwar, wild-camped and cozied up under blankets by a great fire, next to which we dried our clothes on sticks.

We gathered firewood just as we had when we had first met, and he brought me coffee just as he used to do every morning, handed to me with a tender kiss.

We celebrated a year of being in each other's lives and toasted to the end of us, as horribly painful as we knew it would be, holding each other close. The time we spent together in the wild will always remain one of the most thrilling and romantic journeys of my life.

THE MAJOR

He was wearing a Pagri, or turban, and his moustache was handlebar, waxed and curled at the edges, his beard full and groomed, a gorgeous silver Sikh bangle on his wrist. He would have looked smart from the neck up, save for his black nylon tracksuit top and trousers, a heavy gold necklace, and white trainers. He was off duty. His name was Major Guggan, and he was inviting us to tea.

It wasn't really an invitation; more of an insistence from all the men at the ground level, at the barrier and the ones holding the fraying rope across the dirt track, our gateway to freedom. Despite our claims of darkness coming and of having tired road-beaten eyes, we were slowly ushered up to a hollowed-out, barely levelled concrete platform on which the Major strode about, steel dumbbells in the corner of his playground. All that was missing was a chained-up tiger.

Plastic chairs and a plastic table adorned with a tea-set lay waiting for us. The Major surveyed us from a height, and as we set eyes on the tracksuit, John said out of the corner of his mouth,

"If this guy keeps us more than five minutes, wearing that..."

After three checkpoints on the same piece of road and identical conversations with three lots of military police, things had become a little cynical and jaded. We were on the edge of Kishtwar National Park, trying to find a wild camping spot for the night, and facing a barrage of questions which we could not answer. My Hindi had improved, but it was proving futile because of course, in Kashmir they also spoke Urdu, among other languages.

After replying to their many questions, the rigmarole of doing this every time just to cross a line in a district had become something of a chore. However, one Punjabi officer, The Major, with both hands in his tracksuit bottoms, despite his crimes to fashion, was an excellent English speaker.

Why were we there? What interest did we have in this road? How did we come to know about it?

Apparently, everyone in Kishtwar now knew our where-abouts. Only that morning, an army official had knocked on the door of the hotel room to enquire about our ongoing journey and sat us down for an official interview. Now we were being stopped once more.

Were we being hunted?

It quickly became clear that we had unknowingly stepped into some territory where there were several wanted criminals from an Islamist militant group that were still at large and who were suspected to be hiding in the area. Although it wasn't funny, I laughed, because our impending detainment for the night at the army barracks was not quite the way I had imagined spending my 33rd birthday morning, waking up to khaki and corrugated metal.

My eyes flashed to a poster on the rock wall outside the mess tents, with six grim-looking figures on it. 'Wanted:

Alive or Dead', the poster read in English, along with a reward for capture. Two were crossed out, with large X's, presumably dead. Another was smeared across the face with some sort of brown paste, which I assumed, in disgust, was faeces.

We were told emphatically not to wild camp, as the neighbouring villagers could be informants to any terrorists who wished to attack a foreigner. We were urged that the road back was not safe in the dark, and that the forest behind their barracks, should we wish to pitch our tent, could be accessed but that he would send his troops first, to personally scour the area for us, to clear it of possible danger.

We looked at each other in disbelief. We had stuck our finger on a map and had had full faith in our gumption, we had followed a broken road, full of holes and dips and cracks and crevices, sand and gravel and tar and sharp stones. We had loaded up the bikes, ingredients for a soup made over a smoking campfire already in our packs and in our minds. Never had we envisaged that we would be being protected by the Indian Army, to keep us alive.

We chose to drive back in the dark rather than face a night in an army barracks, excited by the prospect of driving with dodgy headlights on crumbling roads and devastating drops. As I swung my leg over Ullu, I looked at the men who had big smiles on their faces, waving emphatically. We bade them goodbye with the foreboding presence of the Major overhead looking down on us, kick started our Enfields, and thundered away from the watchful eyes of the military.

Later, we obtained mobile phone reception, curious to know more. We researched the Major's claims. He had been correct. Less than month before our trip, it seemed they had found two members of terror outfit Hizbul Mujahadeen in a hideout in the forest near to where we were. The military presence no longer seemed so tiresome, and as we reminded ourselves of our privilege of being in a very remote border area of India as two white foreigners, we also reminded ourselves that these were not our politics, this was not our business, and we knew very little of it all. We were more patient with the military after that.

WILD CAMPING

We meandered along various rivers and valleys, arriving at a remote Kashmiri village that looked like it had been born from the pages of an adventure journal. A glossy spread of crisp green fields, fir trees, and a river of such pristine turquoise-blue that it sparkled like crystals in the morning sun.

I popped my head out of the tent to see my lover stirring the embers once more, as two wild horses munched on apples from the small orchard that we had camped in. We bathed in the stream, washed pots with rocks, and prepared a simple soup over the roaring fire with a pocketknife, vegetables, and a chopping board made of driftwood. We stowed our perishables in a tree to deter the bears, looked for firewood along the banks, and sat with our knees to the flames.

The next night, we found another spot, between heavily bouldered roads where the rushing water flowed through, with enough dry firewood to keep a village warm. We hung our washed clothing up to dry and drank hot chocolate while we lay naked together under blankets. I looked up to watch the stars and felt time stand still there. We were completely and utterly alone in the wilderness, with cries of wild things in the distance, and I thought to myself that I had never in my life seen so many stars in the sky, nor ever felt this vital and alive.

John slept with a weapon under his pillow, and I jumped uneasily at noises in the darkness. When I got up to urinate in the night, he diligently checked for wild animals; in the Himalayas at night and so close to the riverbed, it was very possible, but we were fortunate that night and there were none.

As the morning sun hit our little tent, we lay in the morning glow, reading on the top of rocks and basking in the heat in the crispness of the wintery morning. As I watched him put his hand, wrapped in the river-soaked hat from his head, into the flames of our fire to pull out a pan of boiled water for our morning coffee, I laughed. I was full of admiration for his independent, practical nature. As I dismantled the tent and we carried our own bags back onto our bikes, I felt him watching, and I turned around to see him grinning at me. It was the same grin that he gave me when I made it up a tricky incline or negotiated the price down in a hotel. I knew he felt the same way, that we complimented one another. It was an alarm bell of a realisation that neither of us had really had a true teammate before, without compromising some of ourselves for another. This was a rare love.

"He's leaving," I reminded myself, as I hugged him tightly for a moment, as my stomach did backflips. He kissed me with great passion and held me closer to him, a knowing look in his eye. We turned our ignition keys, both of us a picture of the road, smelling strongly of campfire smoke, and I ran my fingers over my lips as if to seal in his kiss.

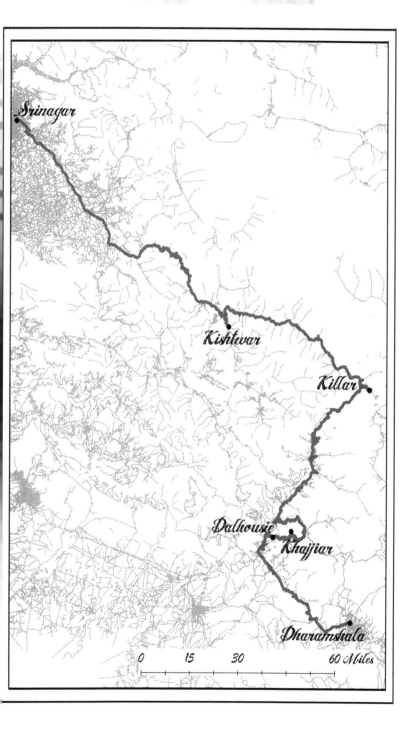

THE CLIFFHANGER

They called it The Cliffhanger. This off-road route joins the forests of Kishtwar in the state of Jammu and Kashmir, where we currently were, through Pangi Valley in Himachal Pradesh. Known as one of India's most deadly and dangerous roads, it is a real treat for the experienced motorbike rider. This also makes it one of the less travelled routes in the Himalayas owing to the level of difficulty.

The route snakes around a cliff face, giving this road its nickname. The sheer drop on one side could have a rider heading 2000ft down into the mighty Chenab River, should they make even the smallest of errors, making it not for the faint of heart.

Several Indian roads I had ridden on had been touted to be the highest passes in all of India and in fact, the world. Most were rumoured to be deathly, claimed by many leather clad and padded bikers in immaculate road gear, selfie sticks attached to their full face helmets with stickers on their steeds reading names of their latest conquests that season. Each biker I passed on these roads wore the kind of motorcycle gear that makes you look six foot tall and four foot wide, but when removed, revealed either a skinny, tiny Indian or someone who was, in fact, six foot tall and four foot wide. In a land of plentiful chapatis, either was possible.

I had no idea of what I was about to face, having done very little research. My Ullu had made mincemeat of most of the road surfaces I had had the privilege to ride upon and hearing the rumours about this route I still trusted her entirely. I tried to remember the hazards on my journeys through Ladakh and Spiti Valley, such as a thin, silky sand which whipped up into the eyes and made my tires grip-less, snaking across the darkening roads like a subtle cobra.

The Cliffhanger was unlike any road I have ever taken, as it would test me in terms of both skill and strength. I had longed for a road like this, as dangerous as its name, something I would remember for the rest of my life, one that would make a good story if I ever made it home.

I could think of no better birthday gift from the universe. After the setback with the military, I was excited for this road. There is no greater thrill to me than risking your life on high ledges, of pushing yourself to exhaustion, of guiding your bike up the dodgiest of inclines alone, your whole life on your luggage rack, knowing at any moment that a momentary loss of focus, a sweaty gripped mistake, could cost you it all.

Having heard so much about it, I was expecting a little more from the entrance than a digger and a nondescript road marker. It turned out that the road, post-monsoon, was under serious construction and was cordoned off; passage of this road had been restricted to only one hour, twice a day. This only added to the thrill, knowing that we would be managing the end of it in darkness. Ullu's headlight needed an update, her vintage glowing bulb not so reliable at spotting hazards in the blackness, and her wheel fork had cracked on the ascent. A severe lack of mechanics in this wilderness meant a bit of a risk, but I was not deterred.

We waited in a dhaba that would, at the end of the pass, rob me of two days of driving thanks to some sketchy tap water. I met two other bikers that met my earlier description. Their bikes were loaded with the latest technology and gear, but it soon became apparent that they had no idea of even the name of the road they were about to attempt. In fact, they were on a KTM RC 200 and a Yamaha FZ25. Now having never had the privilege of riding either, I didn't know anything, but I suspected that the sports nature of the bikes and their factory issued tyres, made for speed on good roads, could cost them dearly on those slippery corners. I had seen both models stuck in precarious situations previously throughout my journey through India, usually in the mud.

We rode back to the checkpoint post to line up behind a fraying rope with the pristine looking bikers who must have thought us quite alien. We were in waterproof jackets and welly boots, open helmets and scarves, jeans and plaid shirts which were secondhand and dusty. John was on my left, a KTM to my right. They finally let down the rope, and we cheered. I was first out of the gate, grinning wickedly, a woman in the lead on the oldest bike in the group.

It was difficult from the first tyre settling onto crumbling rock. With the other passes I had taken, it took a while to reach the sense of oncoming doom, the parts you wish you had one of those fancy head cameras after all, to capture it in all its glory, not that watching it would ever do this road justice.

After five minutes I was laughing maniacally, my arms already stiff from bracing the handlebars against the tough ground, calling out to no-one that could hear me that, "I'm going to die," with shaking hands. In my mirrors I caught sight of the KTM sliding haphazardly as predicted, from side to side along the terrain, as I quickly refocused my attention on the broken road.

The drops were something else. You know when someone tells you that they have been on a high road, and it was steep? Most western roads have at least a safety rail or signs around the edges, or a lay-by to pull over and take photographs, usually named something like 'Sunset point'.

There were no such signs, railings, or anything else on this road. Whilst trying to get a photo of the cliff I sat at the edge for a second and knocked a rock with my boot. Seconds later, a whole part of the cliff fell off where my foot had been, as I scrambled back, praying my companion had not seen me be so foolish. Falling off the edge because I couldn't quite get the correct angle on a photo did not seem quite as exciting as plunging to my death atop my Enfield. The cliff I had been so keen to capture was one of many stunning examples, overhanging, cavernous, and beautifully shaped, sharp angles and grotesque claw like edges. To drive through and under these was like being a part of some sort of fantasy movie akin to Labyrinth, Lord of the Rings, or Narnia.

There was nowhere to stop and take a photo, for the track was just wide enough for one car and there were only one or two patches where it felt safe to stop to enjoy the mesmerising view. As I ducked under low hanging ceilings of rock, there was little room for error.

Several times, Ullu's wheels left the ground entirely and achieved air space, landing with a bounce that could easily have sent me over the side. My whole body was injected with adrenaline, and I was shaking with a mixture of fear and absolute bliss. I did not dare cast my eyes over the side, where at times mu right foot dangled over the ledge. I kept my eyes steadily on the track, ferociously focused, and could not take my hands from the bars to wipe the sweat from my eyes for fear of slipping, plummeting down thousands of feet, to be lost forever. I did not want it to end.

The road straightened out a little then, and the desert-stone rocky paths made way for lush green forest once more, and suddenly we were riding on luxuriously smooth road, and it was all over as quickly as it had begun, looking for a guest house to spend the night at in Killar. I fought the urge to go back and try it once more time and remembered that night was falling.

The lads on KTM's passed us after some time, and they raced off on the flat, my partner and I exchanging knowing smiles; our Enfields had certainly set the standard. Ullu's cracked wheel fork had held out, with her mudguard to be wrenched off entirely the next morning by a bunch of local surly welders, as it, too, had given up; Cliffhanger had certainly been a test of both rider and bike. We had made it just in time, as night fell.

If I had to choose a favourite between this and the famously deadly Saach Pass, a road which we took two days later, I fell in love with The Cliffhanger. It's like when you get on a roller coaster, and it's just the right amount of fun without making you nauseous; Cliffhanger left me wanting to do it all over again.

I remembered with a gulp all the bikers I had met on the way whose suspensions had given out on roads nowhere near as treacherous and made a mental note to treat Ullu to a new oil change and a good bath when we got home. This Daddi bike had beaten the odds.

SAACH PASS

Saach Pass, also claimed by BRO as one of the world's most dangerous roads, was heads and shoulders above The Cliffhanger in terms of length. It stretched from Killar to Khajjiar, near Dalhousie, and was a very chic place to spend the hot summers, but much colder in October. We were the last ones to do the pass, with only one more day left to achieve it before it closed.

I had been desperate to do this pass but had been warned off doing it from this direction back towards Dharamshala by a seasoned biker gang. They told me over a beer in Manali that I should not do it alone as it was a steep, barren road with no available rescue should my bike fail. As John and I had now teamed up, it was entirely possible with a second biker.

This pass was rumoured to be difficult to do backwards, sometimes icy, or with great banks of sand, which, for bikes going uphill, is about as slippery as it gets. We took a break as soon as we got into the pine tree line, as it was then that the rattling of my mud guard had reached its limit in terms of wobbliness and was now distracting to listen to, so we fixed it a little tighter with a bootlace through the crash guard.

The front wheel fork, on closer inspection, had a huge crack through the centre of it due to impact, thankfully held securely in place by the large bolt. I was hopeful that she would make it down to safety, and in any case, she had to, for there were no mechanics on this stretch whatsoever.

The Cliffhanger had certainly put my Machismo through her paces. I was amazed that Ullu did not have any further damage, having felt her roll and jolt from one uneven path to another, her old twice-welded frame holding on. Cliffhanger had been an incredible ride, and I could not wait to see what Saach Pass had in store for both bikes.

The route differed to The Cliffhanger as it was more tiring; I was still suffering from drinking some bad tap water at the dhaba, so I had not eaten a thing. The ground was so potholed and textured in every way that it was impossible to go quickly, and it became more of an endurance task than anything else. It was mainly uphill, and not quite as bumpy as Spiti Valley, but almost. The sheer duration of it surprised me, and we had not even reached the summit.

The ascent brought many challenges, mainly because of construction. We were not completely alone because of the diggers which took over the entire pass and were impossible to squeeze by, and patience was not something we had in spades because of the time restraints, but we had to wait, as there was nowhere to go. In the end, I took to laying on the horn only for them to shift over merely an inch. We had no choice but to ride on the outside edge, sometimes unsure if there was space between the edges of our cages and their chunky tyres. I refused only once, sensing that the available space was too much of a risk to take, rocks crumbling from the sides where my tyres would have tried to grip, when one tiny bump would have meant the end with the enormous drop below.

Some of those moments passing the vehicles were enough to stop my heart. I look back now and wonder where that bit of bravery came from, and I know that it is only trust in our wonderful bikes that gave us the courage. The most memorable dodging of death culminated in wedging my front tyre between two boulders, as we rounded one digger and began an immediate and slippery uphill climb up some recently dug —up chunks of hillside which measured half of my tyre size. Ullu, true to her name, flew up and over them, losing control finally over one very jagged piece of boulder, landing dramatically into the inner cliff face.

I was so grateful to be up and over that path having had absolutely no run-up, as Ullu had been known to slide back due to lack of power on a hill climb or two, that I did not care that I was now completely stuck in a wall. There had been a split second to think; this route had been completely hidden by the digger. The driver of the digger and my partner pulled me out of the rocks while I laughed hysterically as he told me,

"Aram-se, Didi."

Slow down.

I was amazed that Ullu had made it to the top at all. My partner was on my side.

"Nahin, Ji," he said, and pointed to the route we had taken, shaking his head. To have taken it slowly would have meant absolute failure, sliding down the hazardous bank, and he knew it as well as I did.

"Jaldi, Jaldi," I said. And quickly we rode, up the very next slope, with every construction worker stopping work, wide-eyed in wonder at these two ridiculous foreigners covered in dust, attempting these broken roads on a bike that was making more noise than all their machines combined. Ullu was tiring, her tappets somehow holding on and her engine desperate for a place to rest.

Two slopes later, after we had pushed one bike up at a time on the steepest incline yet, I realised my laptop bag had dislodged itself where I had crashed into the rock, possibly due to a bungee cord that was now completely sliced in two. I thanked my stars that this was not a sliced tyre instead, and John gallantly went back for it so that I could rest my ailing bike.

I can only imagine the faces of those construction workers when he returned. Luckily, India is one of the most brutally honest places I have ever been lucky enough to travel to, and my precious cargo was safe in the arms of one of the men who gave it back gladly.

I soon abandoned my battered bungees for thick rope. In all my trips, I must have been through about twenty of those market-stall bungees, liable to snap at any moment, constantly in need of adjustment, and very badly made. In all the guides I had read on India, I had not yet come across this well-known and essential travel tip anywhere, but it was now one that I would shout from the rooftops to anyone who would listen.

As we neared the top, I saw a great length of the Himalayas in panoramic view. I found myself spellbound again to have seen the vast differences and experienced spell-binding sights that most would never see in their lifetime. I took a quiet moment to walk around a tiny mountain temple, lit with incense though I did not know who was around to do such a task. I asked for safe passage down, my hands together in respect to those who guarded the mountains.

I had learnt to do this in Spiti; many said that because I did not circle the temple in respect on each pass, my bike had come to injury. Buddhists call this circumambulation: a way to shield yourself from misfortune. I was not about to argue with a tradition set by generations of Tibetan and Kashmiri people.

When we did finally reach the sign, it was a bit of an anti-climax; the tent where we had planned to eat was not offering any food at this time, as it was so rarely frequented. Someone had thoughtfully and hilariously parked a digger in front of the pass sign which was just a spray-painted 'Saach Pass 4500m', but as this route was so rarely travelled, I should not have expected any more. I managed to grab a couple of packets of spicy snacks to sustain us and we shovelled them down at top speed.

Only one brand-new Mahindra 4x4 had made it up the pass, filled with families of Indians who were all suffering with altitude sickness. The sun threatened to set within an hour, as we watched the sky separate into an artist's palette of different tones, splodged across the top of the jagged Himalayas. We had timed it wrongly, so the views through the thick forest below would soon fade. Still, I was riding at sunset on one of the most beautiful mountain ranges in the world, and we had completed many tricky roads in the darkness now. One more would not hurt.

The area around the top was frosty and barren, with patches of glaciers which did not match my expectations. Having felt the immense cold on the climb upwards, I had thought that it would all be white. In a few days, it would be impossible to cross it, with thick snow threatening in the clouds above.

Desert-like, I thought, remembering Leh and those surroundings, but it was a desert in the sky. There was a lonely space-like quality to all the passes I had experienced so far, and this was certainly one of the loneliest of all; there was not a sound to be heard. No birds, no streams, no other vehicles. It was heaven in many respects, had the climate not been so harsh to stay for more than a few minutes. I meditated a while on a cliff edge and began to feel heady as I remembered the importance of not staying at the peaks for too long. I fished out a rogue piece of garlic from my pocket and chewed it but did not swallow, allowing it to mix with my saliva and do its work to reverse the sickness.

I was starving now, and the thought of a hot shower and a warm bed was enough to power me down the long descent. John and I were both determined to do some of the pass alone, and with my heavier throttle hand, I set off first on Ullu. The road shingles which had been laid to ensure better grip on the ascent now became more of a hindrance than a help, my mud guard was shaking dramatically, and I worried for the wheel fork.

Down the steep incline I went, shifting my weight onto the back tyre and holding on tightly, having to remove one thick glove and then the other for better grip though my fingers were turning purple. The light turned the road ahead into the surface of a desolate planet once again in deepest crimson, and the sky behind us began to mimic the flames of a great fire. Shadows ran down the valley and made the trees look like deadly black spikes. I wondered how easily our bikes would fare in the fading light, with Ullu's sleepy headlight.

There is something about going downhill that hits all my buttons. The reactivity of your senses, the clutch control as you move down through the gears, and the split-second spotting for hazards as you cruise smoothly round blind corners. This was possibly the most difficult stretch of downhill that I had experienced in my bike journey so far, and I will tip my hat to Saach Pass in that respect.

In the fading light, the hazards were increasingly hard to spot. We hit a few and lurched but did not fall. It was a question of concentration for hours, ignoring the last flickers of golden light to our right as I inched along with quick precision to avoid all manner of deep bumps.

Ullu crossed an intense stretch of mud; the rains clearly had reached here recently, and it looked like a swimming pool of muck. It took my last remaining ounces of strength to guide her through, tyres sliding out left and right, skiing across flat planes of brow. I was covered from head to toe.

There was no time to change and so I decided to stay in my now soaked and mud-caked shoes, and in hindsight this probably kept me warmer, Ullu's overly warm engine heating my feet and turning the liquid inside them to a warm gloop which felt quite pleasant after the chill of the top of Saach.

Finally, the road became somewhat flatter, and I allowed Ullu her first coasting in a while, I felt her engine take a huge sigh of relief, and she quietened.

As I slowed, a dog fox came out of the forest and ran in front of my headlights, his bushy tail majestic. I watched him for a while, grateful to be in such pitch-black wilderness alone. It occurred to me then that there were probably many more dangerous wild creatures than foxes in the thickets, and so I did not stay too long. The wilderness of the Himalayas is a privilege and is unguarded; it is not a safe place to be alone in the dark.

A few minutes later, as I was idly winding down through the silent forest, my intuition slammed into me with sheer warning, and instead of coasting down the road I immediately floored it, heart beating with adrenaline, and I did not look back. India has taught me that when that gut feeling hits you, trust it, and perhaps in this case, looking for the source of that feeling could well have been a daft move. Whatever it was, it was as if it were on my tail, breath on my neck, and whatever it was, I knew only that I was being chased.

John caught up to me and we drove the last few miles

together, towards a comfortable bed and garam pani, hot water, with the hope of our favourite dish of Paneer Bhurji and a well-deserved beer. As we clinked bottles, the reality hit us both of what we had accomplished in the past few days. Two great passes had been completed, surviving fantastic and difficult driving conditions, and we had both come out of it unscathed and with two still-purring Enfields. It occurred to me then that we had done something great, something that we could each be proud of. As I thought back to that woman who first sat on a motorbike only one year ago, little did I know how far I would have come.

HOMELAND

He left, bags on his back and squeezing through the doorway,
leaving his kiss on my lips and his warmth on my hands, my legs
hugged to my chest in a cold bedroom. I couldn't bear to say
goodbye in the taxi; the tears that flowed all the morning were
enough, the squeezing of my guts and pins in my jaw; he will
leave me.

I cried as he cried, as hugs that would never be enough made way to
long kisses that did not let me breathe, salt cascading down my
cheeks. His eyes full of fear, I wonder what mine read back, as my
heart shouted out loud,
"Don't go, my love, don't."

His family are waiting, arms wide for embraces that will feel his
heart beating like I used to, like it was only ever for my ears, a
chest I will no longer lie my head against, I will not kiss this neck,
put his lips to mine again. I return to the unmade bed, crawl into
the covers and under, and wait for the onslaught. The grieving.

Every engine I hear is you turning around, to grab me

and to say, "Quick, pack up, we'll go together."
Every car door slamming is you saying,
"One more day, just one more together."

Every splash of puddle on this corner is you crossing the street, to
run back up these stairs, to bury your head in my hands.
Every creak in the corridor, every dog that barks, each jingle of
keys, the rustling of bags and my insides jump, like little heart
shocks, to get me to open my eyes.

But if I have open eyes, I will see this cold room, this hard floor,
your discarded things in the corner, and the space where you lay in
the bed, the shape of you on the sheets and your shirt I will wear to
go to sleep.

RETURN TO RAJASTHAN

India was asking all the foreigners to leave. It was fair enough. India had allowed us to stay for the pandemic, and had kept us safe, and I was immensely grateful. It was time for me to return to England, to renew my visa, but not before I had seen the desert. I hopped on a train to Pushkar, in Rajasthan, for a spot of sight-seeing and to wait for a cheap ticket back to my homeland.

Ullu was tucked up in a little garage in the mountains next to Pushkarini, after their adventures together. I had winterised both bikes to some success, even stuffing metal wool in the exhaust pipes to ward off hibernating animals, filling them to the brim of their tanks with petrol, and disconnecting the batteries. Ullu would wait for me patiently, until the next time.

The business-rich ethos of the small, holy city of Pushkar made for a very comfortable home in which for me to write and massage. The housing was cheap and was traditional Rajasthani rooms with ornate archways. Every morning I would be up at sunrise to marvel at the view through my window before the rest of Pushkar opened their eyes. Slowly, the town would start to wake up, the scraping of the tin at the corner dhaba and the splash of those who were bathing, or walking clockwise around the lake in silence, as was the custom.

A little stall in the square sold Poha for ten rupees, which was a generous serving of hot and flavourful breakfast rice with spices, fresh coriander, and zesty lemon, served on a scrap of newspaper. The tiny chai stand was owned by a group of men who knew everything about the little city, who sold the packets of peanuts to sprinkle on your poha. Across the square, the family who performed Aarti every evening also owned the dhaba, who knew Suraj my landlord, who knew Navneet the travel agent, who knew Sonu the juice man, who knew Ravi, the jewellery guy. There is a saying in India,

"Sab Kuch Milege," which means, "everything is available". It was true, and it was a huge part of how I had managed to survive for so long in India, having had access to that mentality. I felt many times as if India had a magic wand, and it never grew tired of granting wishes for me. I had only to ask for what I needed, and someone would help, as it was all over India, a reciprocal community. The ladies who sold amla berries earnt very little, but always gave you extra. The Gurudwara fed us every day, no questions asked, and was some of the most incredible food I have ever tasted. The sellers had a 'first customer of the day' rule, whereby you were given a great deal on anything, to bring both parties luck. Pushkar was a stunning purgatory, full of new experiences and kind-hearted Indian people, which brought me back to the spiritual side of India which I knew I could not leave without revisiting.

As the desert nights grew colder, I thought about how

this would be a second Christmas without my family, in a foreign land. Our travelling family was well and truly scattered now, with most returning to their homelands. As I sat on my favourite step of the ghat to watch the sunset, it dawned on me that this land was no longer any more foreign to me than England, India's ways and communities making complete sense to me. It seemed that in India, whether in the mountains or the desert, wherever I placed my feet was always home.

One evening, around Aarti time, I was by the lake, wrestling a plastic bag from the mouth of a cow, when I spotted a troupe of drummers by a Shiva temple, playing traditional Rajasthani drums.

Nagara drums are two in number, and face towards one another with one making a lighter, tinnier, kettle-drum sound and the other a more tribal boom. They are used in folk ceremonies, weddings, and celebrations. Nathulal Solanki, a famous local musician, began to tune one of the drums at his feet, and said to me,

"Nagara are male and female, always talking. Always talking the language of Tabla. The female drum taking a little longer to get ready, as it is in life also."

I giggled at his personification of the instruments. There was the duality again, the symmetry that appeared all over India, and was evident everywhere, if you took notice. I watched the only two swans in Pushkar, love-struck and inseparable, who flew around the Holy Pushkar Lake at night, settle gracefully onto the water as a snake thrashed in the shallows, fighting another.

Nathulal and his entire family were talented drummers, even down to their bachchas, boys who were barely old enough to hold drumsticks. I was given a pair of battered sticks and invited to sit at the lake edge. It became a meditation at every sunset, as we watched the Rajasthani towers create an ink print of a silhouette into a rose-red sky.

Day by day, others began to arrive from my lockdown travelling community, and soon I was with friends once more. Our group of foreigners played the Nagara drums at all sorts of celebrations across the city, at both the delight and confusion of the Indians who watched us. Pushkar's famous camel fair came into town and we dressed in traditional clothing, the men winding two metres of cloth around the heads of their brothers, into a pagri, and the women in beautiful silk saris.

Parades of camels lined the streets, painted with spices. They were dressed up in fabric trinkets with traditional gypsies leading them around with wooden piercings through their noses. Some of the camels were tied by the legs, and the ropes between their two front legs were so short they could only shuffle. I stood by them and pointed for long enough until their owners tutted but released them. Seconds later I was smiling at the other camels being given kisses, lovingly sat with their owners, sharing their chai. India was showing me light and darkness, just as she always had.

The street vendors started to stock spools of string and kites for the famous kite festival, Makar Sakranti. The tourists came back little by little as more and more countries returned to India, and suddenly the streets of Pushkar were no longer as empty, with the home-grown businesses of Pushkar recouping their losses of two years of unfortunate luck.

The winds came, blowing with them the dust of the desert and with that, the arrival of winter. Four pelicans came to settle on the lake, and with them came wedding parties which celebrated late into the night, Bollywood music playing on the breeze. Pushkar was alive once more, as I hoped that the rest of India would soon be.

COOLING THE PITTA

Ayurveda is called 'The Mother of All Healing.' It is a healing science, found in the Vedas. The Vedas are religious Sanskrit texts which focus on the cosmos and are the oldest scriptures of Hinduism. The texts are 'what is heard' by ancient Hindus after intense meditation.

Ayurveda focuses on balancing mind, body, and consciousness, and which many Indians have knowledge of. It maintains that we have three Doshas, or states: Vata, Pitta, and Kapha which can be labelled as Air, Fire, and Earth energies. They believe that these states govern our emotional, mental, and physical characteristics. In the practice of Ayurveda, the body is formed of a unique combination of the three, with one or two predominant energies.

Indians visit an Ayurvedic doctor for a few rupees, who will then feel your pulse, a process called 'Nadi Pariksha,' to decide which dosha you are most dominant in, and if you are currently in 'balance'.

They believe that your dosha is determined at birth, but there can be an imbalance of too much or too little of one dosha, which can change how you act, think, feel, and behave. The idea is to keep these individual imbalances in check, by using diet and lifestyle choices to maintain equilibrium within the body.

If 'Vata' is air and space, it can be emotionally characterised by people who can be worriers or of a nervous disposition, quick movers, and great thinkers, mimicking the elements of air and space.

'Pitta' refers to fire and water, and can be characterised by energetic, gutsy, and confident people, prone to anger and impulsiveness. As I was known as a 'Pitta' type, I was told to lower my coffee intake and spice to keep my fiery qualities at bay when I was feeling out of control. I refrained from these for one whole year after meeting Gagori, a celibacy from stirring my own flames.

"She knows it is the coffee, but still she drinks the coffee. Always we look to punish ourselves because we are addicted to our own pain."
- Gagori

I did not believe myself to have had a sprinkling of 'Kapha'. I found earthy, water-loving Kapha-dominant people to be my closest friends in India, gravitating only to those who made me feel as close to this calm feeling as possible. Many people say that India in general 'feels' like Kapha energy, and that wherever you go in the world, India is wired differently, that there is something in the Indian soil that grounds you and calms you. Some say it is lazy, or slow, but I knew that I could live my life in a way that connected me to that deep grounding feeling, a steadiness.

It is easy to see how my life in England did not suit me. Living a life of high stress and deadlines, within a generally fast-paced society sent my nervous system into overdrive. I had developed anxiety; I was unregulated and struggling.

India had turned out to be my saviour, forcing me to slow down so many times that eventually even my speech and physical movements slowed their quickness, and my patience reached an unprecedented level.

I remembered my first Ayurvedic experience back in Rishikesh, with a doctor of Ayurveda, when he had felt for my pulse and pronounced me,

"Pitta. Bahut Pitta." A lot of fire.

I had asked him what that meant, and he had just smiled, and said that I was exactly where I needed to be. I knew what he meant; Gagori had told me that I had a Vata imbalance, and this meant that perhaps I finally had it under control.

When a second doctor, after a year of living in India, pronounced me Pitta-Kapha, I almost jumped for joy. The Vata of two years ago seemed to have finally been placated, the whirling thoughts in my head had settled like the Ganga after Monsoon, and the helpless cycle of being at war with myself seemed finally to have been broken.

As I wandered the narrow streets of Pushkar wondering if the Indian government would grant me permission to stay for my third mango season, I suddenly noticed I was able to withstand the noises of the streets without letting them overwhelm me; I wondered how long ago that had happened, and why I was only noticing it now. I laughed out loud at the tinny old loudspeakers on a cart being wheeled through the streets at top volume, playing temple music.

I sat down to drink a juice on a busy street corner and took in the electric chaos of the street. I grinned at the beggar children running from an old Sadhu they had woken from his sleep, and at a cow and her calf inches away being fed scraps from a table. An auntie was chiding her husband and a monkey was clattering on the wiring above. Sitting here amongst it all was as easy as breathing. India had broken me and put me back together again, in the best way.

"It is not that we are noisy, it is that we do not know what is silence."
- Pushkar seller

KITE SEASON

A kite flies with the wings of a bird. Swallows flit across orange skies, teasing the diamond shaped paper edges back and forth with their wingtips, like courtship. As Rajasthani flutes swell the air, the kites dance and sway their hips on the undulation of every note, rising with the drone of Sarangi violins. Sunset burns a red ball of fire between temple tops and winding streets, and the blue ceiling of a sky is suddenly awash with bright paper patterns, two simple sticks and a reel of cotton string. A flurry inhales them all in a rush, up they go, one and then another, caught in the wind's laughter.

They play tricks; a child tries to cut through the string chasing the other like a devil through the skies, two playmates locked in a fierce embrace, until one is knocked asunder, spiralling to the ground, it spins in the wind, helter-skelter. Drums sound in the distance, and for a moment, the soft rippling sound of fluttering kites is the only sound in the sky.

As Aarti bells ring, the kites are flying still. Until the last breath of wind blows, until there is no light to see nimble fingers catch cotton, expertly throwing their toy from side to side.

And tomorrow, when another cool breeze arrives, and the birds signal that it is time, there will be multiple tiny footsteps, running up the crumbling stairs to the bare rooftops of the city, to try to catch their prize.

FULL CIRCLE

December.
As the warm sun squeezes through tiny patches of awning, the
shade is cold in the baking days and bitter nights in the deserts of
Rajasthan.
As the sun sets on Pushkar Lake, I shiver and watch the sky, yellow
butter spread with amber. Langurs chase each other and chatter,
dangling on old telephone cables and fourteenth-century parapets,
crumbling into dust with age and heat. The sky is full of circling
birds, each borrowing the wind of another as they swirl and dip in
perfect unison, before settling once more onto the ghats. Within
moments they are off again, into the purpling sky, winding around
the bats that catch the mosquitoes, shimmered reflections dancing
underneath them, the lake water like a shiny silver mirror.

This is India, I thought, as I threw white jasmine flowers into
the lake and watched the flickering flames of Diya lamps
light up the ghat, the smell of oil burning on the water.

This is India, I thought, hearing voices chanting, a myriad
of instruments clashing, deafening and yet pulling at my
insides with their raw emotion.

This is India, I thought, as graceful women in saris and red lipstick knelt at the rose-petalled water of the lake. I stepped down the ghat in bare feet to join them, shoulder to shoulder, singing, milk-skinned in a sea of caramel faces, hennaed feet and bindis shining.

Mothers and daughters grasped my hands in theirs and took me to dance in circles around a single flame, for an auspicious day, the celebration of a Goddess.

The moon slips out from behind an ash-grey cloud. It is full and bursting, majestic, challenging the sun in its brightness. As one lone cow lies down to sleep on the temple floor, the bells ring out and the Aarti lamp is lit. They sing, pouring milk from silver jugs into the bath, throwing petals, cold toes at the water's edge.
Sadhus light fires in the street, the thick smoke winding up into the cold night air, to mingle with the smell of chana dal in the market square roasting on an open flame. Blankets cover shoulders as they make their way home across cold desert sand, as lights flick on one by one in alleyway windows, and street dogs wag their tails with excitement, ready for another evening of howling at each other, and at the moon.

ABOUT THE AUTHOR

Waiting for Mango Season was born in a rooftop café in Rajasthan, overlooking Pushkar lake. Ellie penned her chapters to the sound of aarti chants, chattering monkeys, temple bells, and her favourite blues and folk music.

Ellie is a singer songwriter from York, UK. She performs with and writes lyrics and melodies for country-folk outfit Gilded Thieves.

Ellie writes evocative descriptions of her travels to capture the significance of her experiences. Her poetic prose style is a lament to the people and places who have shaped her, her accounts told with whimsy, wit and grace.

When she is not writing, Ellie is usually travelling solo or learning new skills. A trained massage therapist, Ellie works with somatic bodywork techniques. She is also a silversmith, creating bespoke designs inspired by the Himalayas.

ACKNOWLEDGMENTS

Thank you to everyone who has contributed to this book. Waiting For Mango Season does not only belong to me; it was inspired by the many travellers I shared my days with and the Indians who all became family, and India herself, for the very nature of her land and all that she taught me. Dhanyavaad, bahut dhanyavaad. I will never forget what you have done for me.

To my friends and editors Malina, Sophia, John, Pippa, and Jane for their thoughtful insights, to the formatting wonder that is Rob, and the outstanding talent that is Emma Abel, illustrator. I created an audio version with the wonderfully patient Liam, plotted maps with Katherine, and borrowed many beautiful voices to tell this story. I could not have done this alone, so thank you all for being a part of it.

Thank you to those who followed my journey and to anyone who has supported me by buying a copy of this book. I am so grateful to each one of you for helping me realise this dream.

To Gagori and Nikhil, my teachers. Thank you for awakening me to my patterns, without you I may never have broken through. You are magic.

To Liesl, my guide. Thank you for answering questions with more questions, and for giving me eyes when I have been unable to see. Your work is vital.

To Laul, Cait, Alex and Rachel, my constants. Thank you for being my rocks.

To my Ullu, for giving me wings.

GLOSSARY

Aarti :
A morning and evening devotional ceremony for the Gods and
Goddesses, and is also said to remove darkness and obstacles. The largest
are performed next to the water of the Ganges in the pilgrimage or holy
cities such as Haridwar, Rishikesh and Varanasi, with smaller celebrations
in other cities with rivers and lakes. It can be done in temples or in homes.
It includes offerings of fire in the form of ornate lamps or plates with
candles which are circled by Hindu priests. Sometimes milk is poured
into the water and there is ringing of bells and other instruments, and
bhajan (songs) depending on location and the celebration. Diya with a
candle and flowers are also floated down the Ganges river. At the end,
devotees cup their hands over the flame and put them to their foreheads
to receive the blessing. The most famous are the Aarti at Varanasi,
Rishikesh and Haridwar, the three holy cities of India.

Anja:
A chakra point, the 'third eye', a centre of intuition and insight, said to be
connected to the pineal gland in the centre of the brain. Many spiritual
practices focus on 'opening' the third eye, to gain higher spiritual knowledge and wisdom.

Ashram:
A holy space, where sadhus, yogis and teachers study Sanskrit texts, practice yoga and meditation, and teach others this practice. Some charge
money for foreigners to stay there, others are completely free, and some
insist on 'Dharma Yoga', which means you volunteer time to certain tasks
such as scrubbing floors or painting, to help the Ashram. Many people
stay for extended periods of time to fully immerse themselves in the spiritual practices.

Auntie :
A term of affection and respect for a woman who is older than you, or
someone whom you do not know.

Aum:
The 'universal sound', believed by Hindus and Buddhists to be the first

sound that was ever made by the universe, a divine vibration. A sound of peace, it is chakra-aligning and meditative to chant this. It is first mentioned in the Vedic texts, Upanishads and used in the Jain religion, chanted as part of five syllables. Buddhists chant 'Om Mani Padme Hum'.

Ayurveda:
In Sanskrit, this means 'The Science of Life' and is over 5,000 years old. It is a holistic healing system developed in India based on balancing mind, body and spirit. It is a form of complementary or alternative medicine. Ayurveda maintains that every person is made of five elements; fire, space, air, water and earth, which combine to make your individual dosha, which is Vata, Pitta, or Kapha. Your dosha can be found by visiting an ayurvedic practitioner. An Ayurvedic practitioner may perform a Panchakarma, which is a cleansing process, to reduce symptoms which are 'out of balance' and to restore harmony in the body. You can lessen or worsen your natural traits and afflictions within the body by your diet and by performing lifestyle changes.

Baba:
A term for an older man meaning 'father' or 'grandfather'. Some also use this to refer to someone who is spiritual, for example, someone who feeds the same Sadhu every day may refer to them affectionately as Baba.

Bachchi:
A little girl, Bachcha: a little boy.

Bahut:
Very, a lot. Eg. Bahut Dhanyavaad (Thank you very much)

Banyan Tree:
These are sacred trees to Hindus and Buddhists which appear in many scriptures and are said to be immortal, as they can live for many years. They can grow laterally as much as several acres and are known as 'walking trees' as their roots form new trunks, which sprout new aerial roots. Holy persons will often live underneath or near them, and monks will pray in front of them, believing the trees to be the place where deities visit. People visit to present the trees with offerings, placing photos of deities in the roots, or wrapping kautuka string around the trunk which is blessed. Often confused with Peepal trees, they are part of the same family, but Banyan trees have long vines or aerial roots which hang down, and their trunks are particularly gnarled and twisted. The most famous Peepal tree is the Bodh Gaya, where it is said that Buddha sat underneath

and meditated and achieved enlightenment.

Bindi:
Worn on the forehead or Ajna, the third eye. In some parts of India, girls will wear this, but it is predominantly married women who will wear a red dot of vermillion powder or a press-on jewel between their eyebrows, symbolising love, and strength.

Brahma:
Creator of the Universe in Hinduism. He is one of three creator Gods including Vishnu and Shiva. He is depicted with no weapon, unlike other male Gods, and is sitting on a lotus.

Chadar tent:
A small temporary or season-only tent or metal house on the side of the road in the Himalayas. Usually frequented by truckers, travellers sleep next to each other in sleeping bags and blankets, and rise at the earliest possible time to continue on the road once more. It usually includes a hot meal and a chai and was about 200 rupees a night.

Chakras:
This means 'wheel' in Sanskrit. It is believed that there are seven energy centres in the body which energy can rotate through. Energy should flow through all of them equally, but they can get blocked, and cause pain in the body and obstacles in life. The practices to release them include crystal work, asana, breathwork and chanting. Chakras refer to the energy body as opposed to the physical and engaging in energetical practices are said to bring you closer to the energy of the Cosmos.

Chapati:
Also named roti, this is a thin bread which you would eat various meals with, torn with one hand and used as a scoop. For those who are very poor, chapatis are sometimes a daily meal, with little else.

Chaturanga:
A yoga move, usually in a transition from downward dog to upward dog.

Chillum:
A clay or wooden smoking pipe, which is filled with hash, opium or charras, and one hand is held over the end to keep it smoking. It is rough and coarse on the throat. It is said to have been a smoking pipe of Lord Shiva

and to put it to your forehead is an offering to the Hindu God.

Dal Lake:
A lily-pad topped lake, with views of the Kashmir mountains. A main source of income for many people of Srinagar are the exquisite house-boats where you can stay for a night on the water. You can take a Shikara ride and see the beauty of the floating markets.

Damru:
A drum said to generate spiritual energy and represents the cosmic sound of Aum, the first sound of the universe. A pandit will play it during Puja. It is also used in Tibetan Buddhism for meditation.

Devi: Goddess, divine.

Didi: Sister

Dhaba:
An eating house, sometimes just a hole in the wall filled with an outside/inside kitchen, with a few chairs and tables. Usually a few similar dishes are cooked in these and you don't order like you would at a restau-rant. The larger dhabas have menus and you can order what you like, which is safer, because it will be cooked fresh. Himalayan dhabas, or chadar tents, sometimes only offer maggi noodles and drinks, because supplies do not easily make it up to the highest parts.

Ganges :
India's Holy river, which stretches from the Himalayas all the way through India. It is often known as the vein or heart line of India. In India, they pronounce it 'Ganga'. Hindus and Buddhists bathe in this river to purify themselves as it is believed that the Ganga washes away sins and cures illnesses. Ganga is also said to help those on the path to spiritual enlightenment. The Ganges fluctuates in cleanliness, from the clearer mountain waters of the Himalayas to the polluted waters of Varanasi until its end at The Bay of Bengal. It also has cremation ghats at many places where relatives can throw the ashes of their loved ones into the water, to bring them closer to Moksha, or liberation. Also known as Ma Ganga, Ganga Maa.

Ma Ganga/ Ganga Ma/ Gangaji:
A personification of the River Ganges, a Goddess. Considered to be the

life blood of India, Ganga is called upon to wash away the sins of devotees and she is placed in the mouth of those who are dead or dying to purify them. Ganga is celebrated as such festivals as the Kumb Mela.

Himachal Pradesh:
The northernmost state of India, bordering Jammu and Kashmir, through which the Himalayas run. Famous for apple orchards and for being the gateway to the Himalayas and Ladakh.

Julley:
Greeting, meaning either 'Hello', 'Thank you,' or 'Goodbye' in Ladaki, and is a mark of respect.

Ji:
A term of respect, and something you may call someone whom you do not know. Ie, "Namaste, Ji," and can be added onto phrases such as "Bhai" (brother) to mean 'respected brother' or Mata (respected mother) or even Baba Ji (if you know a holy person or sadhu very well)

Kali:
The Goddess of Destruction, often described as a black or blue figure who sticks out her tongue. She represents nature at its most untamed. In recent years she is becoming an icon for women and femininity owing to her ability to present herself as an unapologetic raw feminine force.

Karnataka:
A state on India's West coast known for its rich culture, flavourful food, diverse culture, Islam and Christian influences, and Ayurvedic medicine and practices. Famous for the backwaters, an area of natural beauty.

Kapha:
Earth and Water. In balance, Kaphas are calm and loving. Out of balance, Kapha are thought to be greedy and envious. Kaphas can balance themselves by keeping active and avoiding heavy food.

Killar:
An overnight stop at the beginning of Saach Pass. Saach Pass can only be taken in good weather as it is a long road to cross when you are battling the elements, so often nearing Monsoon time, many tourists will stay in this village until the roads are clear to attempt it.

Kishtwar:
Kishtwar is next to Kishtwar National Park, making for some very scenic driving through large pine forest. It is also the start of the 'Cliffhanger' (Kishtwar to Killar) route which is still relatively unknown, or undertaken.

Khichdi:
A mix of mung lentils and rice, said to cure a person of stomach complaints, and is an ayurvedic food as it is nutrient rich and easy to digest.

Kurta:
Kurta/ Kurti – A long-sleeved tunic which protects modesty and against the heat and is a staple of Indian dress for both women and men. It can be long or short but always covers the behind on women. They are all kinds of colours and patterns and materials depending on occasion.

La:
This means 'pass' in Tibetan.

Langur:
A type of monkey with a long tail which can grow to be very large and powerful, though many are very gentle.

Goddess Lakshmi:
Goddess of wealth and prosperity, beauty and fertility.

Laxman Jhula:
The name of the suspension bridge between Tapovan and Jonk. Jonk is also referred to as Laxman Jhula, which connects to Ram Jhula, and both sides of the bridge have markets and eateries. People bathe and worship by the banks of the Ganges. Sadhus visit here every year on various pilgrimages, and many have made this their permanent home. Aarti is held by the Ganges every morning and evening. As this is a holy city, long layers of clothing and refraining from drinking alcohol and eating meat is advised. Above the river in the jungle are stunning waterfalls, and many excursions are available.

Leh:
11,562ft high, Leh is the joint capital of Ladakh, also nicknamed 'The Roof of The World'. It is a bustling town where they speak mainly

Ladakhi. From Leh, there are many day trips available, such as Nubra or Zanskar Valley, or Spiti Valley on returning to Himachal Pradesh. Beauty spots such as Pangong Tso and Tso Moriri are a day's ride away, and there are many monasteries in the region to visit, such as Hemis and Thiksey.

Machismo:
4-stroke, 1 cylinder 346cc motorbike made between 2004 and 2009 which has been discontinued.

Manali:
A popular hill station to escape the summer heat of the cities, Manali has scenic views of the Himalayas and is the first stop on the route to Leh, on the Manali – Leh highway.

Mango season:
From late March to June, Mangoes grow all over India and it is highly celebrated. The most expensive are the Alphonso mangoes. The mangoes vary in size, shape, and colour, and there are also sour mangoes, which are used to make pickle. Mangoes are often plentiful and can be bought cheaply. Mangoes are the national fruit of India.

Manikarnika Ghat:
The biggest funeral ghat in Varanasi also known as The Burning Ghat. It can be viewed from the river itself, or by sitting next to it, but you must not take photos there. There are a series of rituals which must be performed before someone is burnt in the open air, such as wrapping the body in orange cloth, pouring water on the body from the Ganges, and setting the body alight with ghee. The family then returns for the ashes in 13 days during which a number of rituals are performed. There are different levels of funeral pyres, according to your caste and what you can afford; some people are burnt on the floor whilst others are burnt at the top of the ghat. People who are holy, such as babies or pregnant women, are buried or put into the river instead, with weights attached. If you are bitten by a cobra, you cannot be burnt. The soul is said to escape through the top of the skull and families wait to hear it. If it does not pop during the cremation, the eldest son must split it open.

Mantras:
Phrases or chants used in meditation, healing, and worship. Many mantras are said 108 times, said to correspond with the number of changes in the moon and planets, and also to bring yourself into harmony with the vibration of the universe.

Mehndi:
A form of body art using natural dye in a cone to create patterns on feet and hands. It is a sisterly gesture, and most used for celebrations and marriage rituals. The Indian patterns include peacocks and lotus flowers. There is a folk ballad which when sung, says, "Oh, my beloved…it is for you that I adorn my hands."

Monsoon:
The rains that come after summer, or the wet season, and many parts of India turn a lush green. The rains last for three months and are torrential, causing flooding. Depending on where you are in the country, it is experienced very differently. The hill stations are excellent places to wait out the monsoon as they are cooler, but travel can be restricted in Monsoon. Monsoon is considered to bind India together as it waters the crops and many will pray to Indra, Goddess of weather.

Monsoon Fever:
Once a year in India, a sickness comes from the monsoon rains. Many Indians do not drink the tap water in this time, yet many still get sick and name it this. Many people get ill from drinking or bathing in infected or polluted water and bacteria, and mosquitoes multiply in the vast floods, carrying dengue or malaria.

More Plains:
A flat 15,400ft flat plateau, after Pang. Stunning vistas, green valley, and open skies, with a panoramic view of the Himalayas. A photographer's dream.

Mughal:
An early Islamic Empire from Asia, who ruled for two centuries and brought architecture such as The Taj Mahal and the introduction of the Islam religion to India.

Musk Deer:
An Indian deer which carries a pocket of scent on its belly, but it has been poached to almost extinction.

Nandi:
Shiva's bull, a deity who guards the Shiva temples, If you place two fingers on his horns, it is said that you may more easily view the Shiva Lingum at many temples, and that you will receive a 'diluted' power through this 'window'. It is also encouraged to whisper secrets to Nandi and wishes.

Nubra Valley:
It is made up of two valleys and two rivers, Nubra and Shyok. It is a meeting point of two cultures, Buddhism and Islam, with the border to Pakistan being in Turtuk.

Nullah: (pronounced nallah)
A water crossing, sometimes very deep due to the ice melting and flowing down the mountains in the Himalayas, gathering in pools on the road. The currents are sometimes strong, and many have sand at the bottom and sharp rocks which can puncture a tyre or cause motorcycles to get stuck. It is advisable to pack rubber boots to put on before crossing these, and waterproofs, because even in August temperatures, if you get wet and then cross the high mountain passes, you may get very cold indeed, and there is little in the way of warm shelter to dry your clothing.

Pandit:
A scholar or learned person who performs services to and for the temple, educating others on the rites and ceremonies which take place.

Pang:
A suitable stopover for the night when travelling on the Manali-Leh Highway, in a chadar tent. A chadar bed for the night can cost as little as 200 rupees and comes with blankets and pillows. Travellers will sleep in close quarters or in private iron huts if available, but the former is infinitely warmer, being in closer proximity to the stove. There are no shops, mechanics or anything other than basic provisions there.

Pangi Valley:
One of the most remote areas in Himachal Pradesh, it is full of natural beauty and imposing scenery. It is connected by Saach Pass to Chamba Valley and has many exciting roads to drive on.

Pangong Tso:
Meaning, 'Long narrow, enchanted lake' in Tibetan. One of the highest lakes in the world at 13,862ft, it is claimed by three countries: China, Tibet, and India. You can camp there overnight in a chadar tent. If you drive back via Changlang La Pass at 17,688, it is high altitude and a tricky ride.

Pani Puri:
Small round crispy fried bread into which is poured lime juice, potato and

a spice mix. Usually spicy, and taken in the mouth whole. Also called Golgappa.

Paneer bhurji:
Scrambled cheese with turmeric, spices and herbs, served with roti.

Parantha:
fried roti with smashed potato and chillies inside, usually eaten with pickle or curd.

Parvati Valley:
An ethereally beautiful area that follows the Parvati River, including the hot springs of Manikaran, and it is the end of a Sikh pilgrimage.

Pitta:
Fire and Water. In balance, Pittas are said to be intelligent and understanding. Out of balance, Pittas could be angry and jealous. Pittas can balance themselves by eating cooling, non-spicy foods.

Pranayama:
A series of exercises with the breath which are said to clear physical and emotional obstacles in the body, which releases and harnesses the flow of prana, or life energy.

Punjab:
A state predominated by Sikhs and many speak Punjabi. Their religious epi-centre is Amritsar, The Golden Temple, revered in a similar way to Varanasi. Sikhs wear a steel bangle to remind them of their devotion to God. Sikhs worship in a Gurudwara, which feeds many people every day, and all are welcome; Sikhs give to charity often.

Pushkar:
The Holy city of Pushkar is in Rajasthan, and has a Holy Lake. It is situated in the desert, and experiences cold winters and hot summers. It is a wholesale market for fabrics, silver, gold, crystals and soft furnishings and is popular with travellers and businesses.

Pushkarini:
A stunning example of Vijayanagara architecture, a stone bath with steps leading into it, where people would wash next to a temple.

Ram Nam Satya Hai : 'The name of God.'

There are many reasons why Hindus chant this while they carry the body of a loved one. It is said that they want God's name to be the last words they hear. It is also a comfort to those who are carrying them, and believed to be a way to connect the deceased to God in their dying moments or as their soul leaves their body.

Rangoli:

Patterns made with spices, rice flour, flower petals and crushed stones. They are an art form inspired by nature. Patterns are made at the doorways of households to welcome in Goddess Lakshmi, Goddess of wealth and prosperity. It is said to be a symbol of good luck to have them at your door. They also serve a purpose in attracting insects away from the inside of Indian homes, and exercising the mind as it is often a very intricate practice.

Rishikesh:

A pilgrimage destination in Uttarakhand, in the foothills of the Himalayas, one of the three holy cities in India, where Aarti is performed on the banks of the Ganges. Visitors from all over the world come to Rishikesh to seek guidance from practitioners in Yoga, Meditation and Ayurveda and to bathe in the water. Rishikesh is also an adventure capital, with white water rafting, hiking and camps. It is a starting point for famous pilgrimages to Badrinath such as Char Dham.

Rohtang Pass:

Meaning, 'ground of corpses' after so many people lost their lives trying to travel across this pass. One of the most dangerous roads in India, when I visited, we were forbidden to cross it due to landslides.

Royal Enfield:

A classic motorcycle made in India. India ordered these from England for the Indian army, and then partnered with England to make them in Chennai.

Rupees:

Indian currency, also known as INR. At the time of writing, 100 rupees was close to one English Pound.

Saach Pass:

Open mid June to October, Saach Pass closes due to snowfall and poor road conditions. The beginning and end of the pass are in pine forest, and as you climb, the road gets sparser and more open to the elements. It is a tough and lengthy ride, driving through different scenery from snow-capped peaks to snaking mountain paths.

Sadhana:
Sadhana represents the surrender of the ego in both Hinduism and Buddhism, using spiritual practices to do so, such as chanting, asana, prayer, meditation, studying of texts, and worshipping or visualisation of powerful deities. Some may perform a vow at the start, to promise to uphold it. Sadhana can be anything which focuses the mind and leads you towards peace. Its aim is to lead you away from worldly desires and distractions to allow for learning. There are many different types of Sadhana in Sikh, Jain and Buddhist cultures.

Sadhu:
Sadhu means 'mild one'. Their aim is to become universal, nothing and everything, a holy person with no ties to their human life. Sadhus leave their home and family, taking vows of chastity, silence or poverty to reject their earthly desires. They live a life completely dedicated to their spiritual practices. Many are seen begging or walking one of the many pilgrimages of India and Nepal and are respected by Hindus, who give them money or food in return for blessings. They choose to live poorly and some will paint themselves in cremation ash to represent the death of their human life. There are many types of Sadhus of many different subgroups, including Naga sadhus who are naked and live in caves. Sometimes named 'Baba's.

Sarchu:
A suitable stopover for the night, with multiple army convoys doing the same, in chadar tents and temporary dwellings.

Sari:
Cotton or silk, this can be as simple or as opulent as needed and many women will wear these daily. It is elaborately draped and is one long piece of material.

Shanti:
Peace. In conversation it can also mean "Slow", or "quiet". Eg. "All was shanti" or "Shanti, milege (please)"

Shiva:
The creator, destroyer and restorer of the Universe, and representing

both good and evil. Many devotees of Shiva wear red, white, yellow and orange. He is said to live at the top of Mount Kailash in the Himalayas, in a permanent meditation.

Sherpa:
Himalayan people of usually Tibetan descent, who are Buddhist farmers. They often live very high up in the Himalayas.

Shikara boats:
They are the transportation on the famous Dal Lake in Srinagar, and made to travel down the narrow waterways and around the floating river-boats. A very peaceful way to spend a sunrise and to learn more about Islamic and Kashmiri culture from one of the locals.

Sound bowls:
Tibetan bowls which sing when played. They are made from brass, and there are seven different sizes, which correspond to one of the chakras. They are used in opening chakras, for use in sound healing, and relax-ation. Buddhist monks us singing bowls for meditation.

Tantra:
The belief that everything in the universe is interconnected. There are two strands of Tantra, Buddhist and Hindu. Tantra is seen to expand your consciousness through studying of the ancient texts and by applying the principles to your life. It is a complex subject which uses many different practices to reach your 'highest self'.

Tappet rod:
A component on some motorcycles which assists in opening engine valves and rotating the crankshaft, helping to power the engine.

Thali:
A main meal with the same food offered to everyone, and is served differ-ently all over India depending on area. Thali is usually served with a main dish or several, rice or roti, pickle, papad, salad and a sweet. It is supposed to satisfy all the flavours: sweet, salty, bitter, pungent, sour and spicy, as is recommended in Ayurveda. Thali is usually eaten on the floor, with your right hand and roti is usually used in place of cutlery. In India there is often much gratitude for meals and they are an important shared experi-ence with family.

Thiksey Monastery:
Thiksey is a 15th century monastery, home to old and young monks who are schooled here, and there is a Tibetan library. The views from this monastery are sublime and resembles Polata Palace in Tibet. There is a guesthouse where you can stay here, if you get lucky and they have room. Thiksey is under the Gelug sect of Buddhism and has a statue of Maitreya Buddha which is very beautiful.

Thukpa:
Flat fresh noodles, in a hot spicy soup, a Tibetan speciality.

Tuk Tuk/Rickshaw/auto:
Open door small vehicles that take you short distances and often don't have any suspension. Entire Indian families crowd into these sometimes, and it is amazing how many people can fit.

Urdhwavahurs:
Sadhus who perform extreme spiritual practices such as fasting. Their emaciated frames are startling, but many reach a very old age.

Uttarakhand:
A state in Northern India at the foothills of the Himalayas
Varanasi:
this ancient Indian city, also known as Benares, or Kashi, it is the religious capital of Hinduism and is where many people go each year to die. It is said that by going to Varanasi, you 'invite' death, and it is an important pilgrimage spot and religious city for Buddhists, Muslims, Hindus, Jains and Sikhs. You will find temples next to mosques and it is similar to Srinagar in that the city has a large Muslim population as well as Hindu. It is busy, loud, and a sensory dream.

Vata:
Air and Space. In balance, Vata people might be flexible and creative. Out of balance, Vatas could be fearful and anxious. Vatas can balance themselves by avoiding the cold and getting enough sleep.

Vashisht: Famous for the geothermic hot springs in the temple, it is also the gateway to Ladakh and many travellers will stay here before and after a long journey, to revitalize and relax.

Wheel bearing:

These help the wheels of a motorbike to spin. They can become damaged by mud, water or off-roading.

Wheel fork:
This connects a motorcycle's front wheel and axle to its frame.

Zing Zing Bar: Chadar tents are available here, with stunning vistas of the Himalayas. Another rest stop for tourist and military vehicles.

3ac/ 2ac:
A carriage on a train which has beds that you can lie on during your journey. This is a very free system and although you have an assigned bed, if you're on the bottom bunk, people will sit on it until they wish to sleep. For this reason, I usually book an upper.

Diskit

Khardung La Pass

Leh

Thiksey

Tagsti

Pangang Tso

Karu

Upshi

Tanglang La Pass

More Plains

Lachulung la Pass

Pang

Zing Zing Bar

Sarchu

Baralacha La Pass

Darcha

Jispa

Tandi

Chandratal Lake

Keylong

Atal Tunnel

Vashisht

Manali

Kaza

Pulga

0   15   30   60 Miles

If you loved this book, you can help me keep writing about my adventures by leaving a quick review on the book's sales page.

ELLIE COOPER'S NEWSLETTER

Building a relationship with my readers is the very best thing about writing. I occasionally send out newsletters with details of new releases, special offers and other bits relating to my books and life in general.

If you sign up to my mailing list you will be the very first to receive my blog posts.

Sign Up HERE
www.elliecooperbooks.com/signup

I will always welcome conversation and feedback about my work.
Please contact me directly at:
elliecooperbooks.com
ellie@elliecooperbooks.com
www.instagram.com/elliecooper.author/

Printed in Great Britain
by Amazon

20060034R00157